TO INCR

1000 WAYS
TO INCREASE
YOUR SALES

Alfred Tack

CEDAR

A Mandarin Paperback

1000 WAYS TO INCREASE YOUR SALES

First published 1954
Revised Cedar edition published 1979
by World's Work Ltd
This edition published 1990 by Cedar
an imprint of Mandarin Paperbacks
Michelin House, 81 Fulham Road, London SW3 6RB
Reissued 1991

Mandarin is an imprint of the Octopus Publishing Group

A CIP catalogue record for this title
is available from the British Library
ISBN 0 7493 0568 1

Printed in Great Britain
by Cox & Wyman Ltd, Reading

Contents

The
TACK ORGANISATION

is the largest training organisation of its kind in the world. It has twelve thousand client companies in the United Kingdom including many leading names in industry and commerce. Companies in the TACK group market products and services through every type of outlet and provide the up-to-date practical experience on which all training is based.

This practically, together with highly professional teaching methods, has largely accounted for the success and growth of the Training Division, which offers these courses:

■ FINANCE
Finance for the Senior Executive
Introduction to Finance for Managers
Cash Collection and Credit Control
Intoduction to International Commerce

■ MANAGEMENT AND SUPERVISORY
Leadership in Senior Management
The Multi-Discipline Manager
Executive Development
Communication and Negotiation Skills
   for Managers
Motivational Leadership
Effective Supervision
Effective Supervision – Part 2
Effective Office Management
Effective Office Management – Part 2
Profitable Time Management
Executive Decision Making
Recruitment Interviewing and
   Selection
Performance Appraisal

■ COMMUNICATION
Effective Speaking
Effective Report Writing
Better Letter Writing
Better Use of the Telephone

■ SALES
Sales Training
Sales Training – Part 2
Selling to Industry
Selling to Industry – Part 2
Professional Sales Development
Profitable Negotiating
Professional Telephone Selling
Dealing with Customers by Telephone
Successful Territory Management
Selling to Wholesalers and Retailers
Selling Financial Services
Better Selling through Financial
   Awareness

■ MARKETING AND SALES MANAGEMENT
Field Sales Management
Field Sales Management - Part 2
Profitable Sales Management
Introduction to Marketing

■ SPECIALIST TRAINING
Caring for the Customer
Customer Relations for Service
   Engineers
The Executive Secretary
Introduction to Microcomputers
Training the Trainer

In-Company Training is provided in all these areas, specially designed to suit specific client requirements.

Open Courses are run regularly on most of the above topics, with mixed attendance by client companies from all areas of industry and commerce.

THE TACK ORGANISATION
LONGMOORE STREET LONDON SWıV ıJJ

Telephone 01-834-5001

CHAPTER I

One Certain Way to Increase Sales

IT took me twelve years to learn this lesson. Since then, I have been teaching it both to newcomers to selling and experienced salesmen. It has brought me many letters of thanks—letters which have told me that the writer's whole conception of life has been changed—letters from men who have been selling for many years, who have written to say that they never before realised what they were doing wrong. Yet when I explain it to some young man who wants to become a salesman, I can sense his surprise as he says, "Yes, I appreciate that, Mr. Tack. But what about closing the order? Haven't you any simple formula for getting more orders closed? That's something I really need."

I have attended many lectures on selling, during which the lecturer produced his graphs and charts, and took great pride in the symbols he chalked on the blackboard. . . . "Let the salesman equal X; let us assume that the prospect is B. The customer can be Y . . .", and so it goes on. "A shop can be called the ultimate, and a line may be drawn from A to Y, along which the salesman must travel. Let him beware of Z, as he comes here . . ." The pointer goes to the blackboard.

At these lectures you can always tell which members of the audience understand the least about what is happening. They are those who nod their heads vigorously whenever some particularly intricate use of a figure or symbol is made by the lecturer. I am usually one of the chief nodders.

On these occasions, we all like to try to create the impression that we are well up in the higher mysteries of salesmanship. We try to give our neighbours the impression that there isn't much about the statistical side of selling that we don't know. But when all is said and done, sales are not made because a man is able to let his mind equal X, and the power of his hand holding the

7

sample be Y. Generally speaking, a sale is made because someone has the ability to sell himself effectively to a buyer; and
subsequently is able to make that buyer appreciate the many
benefits he will obtain by placing an order.

In a competitive market, it is the salesman who knows the
one RIGHT way to conduct an interview who will win through,
every time.

WHAT HAVE THEY IN COMMON?

Over the past thirty years of selling, I suppose I have met as
many star salesmen as anyone—men who have risen to the top
quickly, and others who have had to fight hard all the way,
before they have reached their goal. They have been men of
varying types and shapes—tall men, short men, fat men, thick-
set men. . . . I don't think the size or the build of a man has any
bearing whatsoever on his sales ability. Some have been
excitable, others quiet, rather meek-looking men; some hesitant
in their speech, others rapid talkers. They have had many
different characteristics and personalities, yet there is ONE
THING they had in common—the one quality essential for all
good salesmen. I will go so far as to say that nine out of every
ten salesmen that I meet do not have this attribute. Very few
newcomers to selling have it. Very few try to achieve it.

HOW I LEARNED MY LESSON

During my first twelve years of selling I tried everything to
improve my sales ability. Like most youngsters, I was nervous
and hesitant to start with.

One young man I was continually coming up against while
on the road always annoyed me. Often, when I was in a queue
waiting to see a buyer, he would arrive and walk straight past
the queue. The buyer would smile at him and—yes, he would
always be seen before us. I was envious of him. He seemed to
have something, so I thought I would copy him. I would become

a high-pressure salesman. I would start bounding up to buyers. I would begin to demand my rights. . . .

My bounds didn't get me very far. The bounds out became far quicker than the bounds in. And as for demanding rights, I soon learned that salesmen didn't seem to have any rights—not so far as a buyer was concerned, anyway.

No, that system didn't work, so far as I was concerned. Eventually, I came to the conclusion that it didn't work too well with the young man whom I had been envying, either, because some years later when I again came across him, he didn't look nearly so smart as he had done in those early days. He was working for a firm of not very high repute, and he didn't seem to have made any sort of a name for himself.

In the meantime, I tried every method I could think of, from punching my hand to emphasise a point, to a rather diffident manner which was meant to convey the impression that I was rather a nice young man and deserved an order. The buyers, however, didn't appear to think that I was such a nice young man, because I didn't get nearly enough orders.

It all boiled down to the fact that what I was trying to do was to put over an act, and my act was not good enough. I made sales all right, but not as many as I should have made. Try as I would I never seemed to be able to reach the top. The reason? I was trying to copy other people and, unfortunately, I was copying the wrong people.

One day I was introduced to a Frenchman named Simon, who was earning a lot of money selling French silks. I asked him if I might accompany him to one or two of his customers, and he readily agreed. I expected to see him acting in a most excitable manner, throwing his hands about, and describing his materials with great enthusiasm. . . . I saw nothing of the kind.

It was while I was with him that I found the answer to my problems. I learned the one thing that I subsequently discovered was common to all leading salesmen—all men who stand above the others:

THEY ARE ABLE TO CONDUCT THEIR SALE IN A CONVERSATIONAL MANNER

With them, it isn't a question of merely selling a product to a buyer; I don't think the buyer is ever conscious of the fact that he is being sold. A conversation takes place during which one man explains in a friendly manner why the other will derive benefits from certain goods. There is enthusiasm all right, the conversation is not drab or colourless, but it is a man-to-man talk.

So there it is. To be a successful salesman—to earn more money, you have to sell in a CONVERSATIONAL MANNER. And I am going to tell you how you can do this. Now don't say, "Is that all? Why, there's nothing in that! That's easy enough. I thought I was going to get something really good out of this first chapter."

You are—something that can definitely increase your income. Let me tell you this, however: To carry out a sale in this way is one of the hardest things in selling.

The simplest acts are often the most difficult to perform. The late Noel Coward, famous for his easy manner on the stage, once said that it took him years to learn how to perfect the taking of a cigarette case from his hip pocket, then extracting a cigarette, and tapping it on the case in a nonchalant manner.

The majority of salesmen are too conscious of the fact that they *are* salesmen. They call upon the prospect or buyer with the knowledge that they have something to sell. They wade into him from the initial approach. They never let up throughout the sale. There they are, sitting or standing, taut and tense, describing their wares, and hoping that the buyer is reacting favourably towards them.

But that is not selling at all. If selling were only that, then business houses would have tape recordings made, which they could send to their prospects instead of salesmen.

AN EASY MANNER CAN INCREASE YOUR INCOME

You can carry out a sale in this conversational manner, if you want to do so. It means that you will have to practise. It may take you three, four, five or even six months to master the art properly. But you can do it. And when you do it, it will increase your sales.

Now, here is the secret. You can only carry out a sale in a conversational manner if you are able to master the art of RELAXATION.

You've got to learn to relax, because until you are able to do so completely, you are unable to make your prospect relax.

Just think about that for a minute or so. It seems easy, doesn't it?

I have watched many sales in progress. I have seen men who want to be successful salesmen sitting bolt upright in their chairs, fists clenched, mouths in a straight line, all muscles taut. . . . And what happens? Within a few minutes the prospect or buyer is getting just as taut and just as muscle-bound. Then, of course, he starts barking out sentences. This upsets and frightens the salesman, so that he begins barking his replies— or else just mumbling them, perhaps. In the end the prospect says, "Well, let me see your samples." The samples are produced, the salesman starts talking about them, and the buyer says, "No, I'm full up to-day. Come another day." And that's that.

This applies just as much to men who have been selling for years as it does to novices. When, however, a salesman has mastered the art of relaxation, and can completely relax himself, he makes the prospect relax too. When both prospect and sales-man are relaxed, a sale can take place in the conversational manner which, in nine cases out of ten, will result in an order.

RELAX YOURSELF. MAKE YOUR PROSPECT RELAX. That is the golden rule for all salesmen.

When you are completely relaxed, you don't feel nervous, you don't feel tense. Another important point—your voice generally drops a key or so. It becomes more pleasant.

Relax right now. Go on, this very second! Put down this book, and relax. You're probably sitting with your legs crossed. You can't relax your leg muscles like that. If somebody were to pick up your hand and let it drop, it would drop in easy stages, instead of just flopping down. In fact, you're not relaxed at all.

That is why I said it will probably take you three, four or

five months to master the art completely. You can only achieve it by practising relaxation every day.

Remember, by educating your muscles to work for you, you will enjoy good health, and you will achieve a stronger personality. But that is not the main idea behind it. The main idea is to enable you to learn to sell in a conversational manner.

THE CONVERSATIONAL TECHNIQUE

Among the many problems with which I have to deal is that of convincing a salesman that the conversational sales technique, brought about by relaxing, is the real answer to his troubles, and is a far better way of increasing sales than any get-a-sale-quickly formula.

Remember this:

1. The conversational technique is the most difficult kind of salesmanship; but it can be learned, and inevitably it brings results.

2. The lack of this technique is just as evident amongst men who have sold for years as it is among newcomers to selling.

3. It does not mean lolling about, and selling in a slovenly manner.

4. It can only be compared with a sincere discussion which you might have with a friend on an important matter. Because you would be talking to a friend, you would be relaxed, in spite of yourself.

5. The star salesman can conduct a sales interview without the prospect realising that a sale is taking place at all. The prospect then *buys*, as distinct from being *sold*.

6. Because relaxation frees your mind as well as your muscles, the conversational technique, if mastered, results in your selling one hundred per cent efficiently.

7. You can sell just as enthusiastically when relaxed as when tense.

It took me twelve years to learn this lesson. You can learn AND PROFIT by it, within a few weeks. Do just that.

CHAPTER II

R.M.A. Can Double Sales

For a salesman to succeed he must have the *right mental attitude*. This chapter will help you to think along the right lines.

WHO—ME?

Have you ever felt injured because someone has suggested that you were not quite perfect?

If you want to be a successful salesman, you must be willing to learn all the time, and say to yourself, "How does this apply to me?"

Here is just a simple test: Everyone knows, for example, that any man in business, salesmen included, should have clean finger-nails. All right. Well, now, look at your own. Then say, "Does this apply to me?"

Here is another: Have you ever said, "If the workers *really* worked, the old country would soon be out of trouble!" You have? Well, remember, when the workers in the factory talk about others not pulling their weight, they could be referring to you.

TO SELL SUCCESSFULLY, YOU MUST BE YOUR OWN SEVEREST CRITIC.

TWO CABLES

In answer to the Government's call to increase the export drive in the shoe and leather trade, a shoe manufacturer decided to play his part in an original manner. He felt that his company had more or less exploited the possibilities of many of the countries throughout the world, but that there was quite a lot of business in some of the smaller isles.

He sent for two of his salesmen, and told them that he was going to give them special assignments. Then he walked to the globe of the world, which was on a table in his office, twirled it round, and pointed to two small South Sea Islands.

"You will each go to one of these islands," he said, "and try to sell our shoes to the inhabitants. You are both good salesmen, and you have been with the firm for years. Now on your way, and come back with plenty of orders."

Both men wasted little time. Soon they were in aeroplanes, hurtling through the air towards their new territories. A few days later, the manufacturer received two cables. The first read: *Am returning immediately stop natives on this island don't wear shoes.*

The second cable was of a different calibre. It read: *Wonderful news stop natives of this island don't wear shoes stop great opportunities stop will be here for at least three months.*

Remember this story. It shows the difference between the salesman with the wrong mental attitude and the salesman with the right mental attitude.

HOUSEPROUD

A little while ago I visited some people I didn't know very well. On entering the lounge I noticed that the cushions on the armchairs and settee had been well sat upon, and nobody had troubled to straighten them out. A dog was curled up on one easy chair, and lots of his hairs were to be seen all over the cloth covering.

Drinks were handed round, a platter heaped with potato crisps was then placed on a low table, and we were told to help ourselves. My hostess left the room to get some cigarettes, whereupon the dog jumped down from his comfortable seat, ate a couple of crisps, and returned to his chair. I can't say I fancied them after that!

I looked for an ashtray to enable me to dispose of my cigarette ash, and was told, "You needn't worry about that here. We believe that a home should be lived in. We don't worry about a little dust, or anything like that. Just drop the ash on the carpet, and work it well in."

I laughed politely; but, quite frankly, I felt much more uncomfortable than I should have done if I had visited a home where the hostess was houseproud, and where I should have been conscious of the fact that it was a crime to drop ash anywhere but in the ashtray.

The ideal, of course, is somewhere between the highly polished, 'Don't touch anything' home, and the one I have just described.

I suppose, really, it all comes down to this: some people are naturally untidy and some people are tidy. It is so very hard to make the untidy person believe that he can, by hard work, become tidy. There is the man who drops his ash all down his jacket, and then says, "I'm always doing that!" What a sign of weakness! It doesn't matter, of course, if he isn't selling anything, or hasn't got to sell himself to other people. But if he is selling, then the habit is a bad one.

High up on the list of *selling crimes* is that of an ill-kept, untidy kit.

Some of the worst offenders in this direction are leading salesmen. The novice usually does try to keep his kit fairly clean—to start off with, anyway. Many leading men, however, feel too important to bother much about the appearance of their briefcase. Yet many prospects must have had the same feeling when looking into a dingy, dusty case as I had when trying to make myself feel comfortable in that haphazard home mentioned above.

Whether you are a newcomer to selling or a star salesman, the rule should be KIT INSPECTION EVERY DAY.

Dog-eared leaflets must be discarded; the outside of the case must be polished so that it shines; folders should be kept in good condition; and so on.

Remember a sale is made up of a hundred and one little things, not just one big thing; and one of the little things which can make all the difference to the result of your call is THE CARE YOU GIVE TO YOUR SELLING KIT.

DON'T FALL FOR THIS ONE

Brown felt depressed. He hadn't taken an order for a couple of days, and he badly needed a break. Walking into a general store and expecting to get a bad reception, he was rather surprised to be well received. He warmed to his task, and was soon selling in an excellent manner.

At last, he was asked the price. He gave it, and added, "You can have the display stand for only two pounds extra."

The prospect didn't hesitate. He snapped, "All right, you throw in the stand, and I'll give you the order."

Brown agreed, but when, subsequently, he telephoned his sales manager and told him what he had done, the sales manager was cross.

Brown said, "It's all very well for you to talk like that, but we sell a high-priced article, and people expect the stand to go with it."

The sales manager said, "You do realise, Brown, don't you, that you're being penalised for being honest. The dishonest way of trading would be for us to add the price of the stand to that of the article. If we did, the prospects would be quite happy at thinking that they were getting the stand for nothing, while, of course, really they would be paying for it. But how about those customers who don't need the stand? We should be charging them for something they weren't buying. That would be dishonest trading. You go right back to that customer and ask him whether he prefers to deal with an honest firm, or a dishonest firm. Tell him what I've told you."

If a salesman is selling extras with his equipment, for which a charge is made, he should never give them away just to get an order. He should explain to his prospect the position regarding the extra charges, in the same way as the sales manager did to his salesman Brown.

LOYALTY

If you cannot give your absolute loyalty to the firm for which you are working—then change your job.

EIGHT EXCUSES TO AVOID

A thousand reports from salesmen were analysed over a twelve-month period, and the number of times various excuses for not selling cropped up are given below:

Due to slump	86
Workers on short time	50
Christmas holidays	140
Summer holidays	70
Easter holidays	35
Taxation due in January	176
No money about	93
Weather conditions	66

The year of this analysis? 1936. If, therefore, you are thinking of making an excuse now, remember that salesmen were making excuses in '36, as they were before that time, and have been since then.

Make up your mind from now on not to look for excuses. The more you try to improve your selling the less need will there be for you to write on your report form 'Things will be better after the holidays'.

HOW FOUR TYPES OF SALESMEN CAN IMPROVE THEMSELVES

How good are you as an actor? Four out of every ten salesmen at least, are perfect actors—unfortunately. They are so good that they mislead everyone. This wouldn't be so bad if they misled people to their own advantage, but they don't. Their acting ability is misdirected, because it is to their own disadvantage.

When a salesman is acting, he is either trying to hide an inferiority complex, or to cover up his inefficiency. No one can help such a man except himself. Driving him will not assist him; no lecture will put him on his mettle; no man-to-man talk will have much effect.

Possibly you are not like one of the salesmen I am going to write about, but, just in case you are, it will pay you to read most carefully about the various types I am going to list. If you feel that you do come under one of these headings, then it is up to you to put things right.

1. The 'Chip-on-the-Shoulder' Salesman

This salesman is argumentative, is easily hurt by either customer or sales manager; he always feels that he is being treated badly, and that others are trying to put something across him. He is cynical, he doesn't like being taught anything new, or being told that he can learn anything about selling.

Now this man puts over his act, not due to inefficiency—he is usually quite an efficient salesman—but usually because of intense, although well-concealed, nervousness.

Although he is a salesman he is frightened of people, and even when he has to see his sales manager he is absolutely on edge because of this weakness.

If you are a 'chip-on-the-shoulder' man, there is only one way to overcome your problem, and that is to learn to relax.

2. The Grumbler

This salesman is always grumbling. His territory is bad; his backing from head office is bad; his equipment could be improved; and his sales manager doesn't know his job.

He doesn't suffer from nervousness; he suffers from inefficiency.

If you are a grumbler, you must improve your salesmanship by being willing to learn, and then you will find your grumbles getting fewer and fewer.

3. The Talker

This salesman cannot stop talking. At any convention he has to be in the limelight; he talks about any subject at great length, and you can't ask him a question unless he replies in the form of a speech.

His trouble, again, strange to say, is due to nervousness. In his early days of selling he tried to overcome this weakness by talking a lot, and by seeking the limelight to show just how unconcerned he really was. The cure once more is relaxation.

4. *The Servile*

This salesman is, of course, the yes-man in any organisation. He agrees, apparently, with everything that is said to him, but in reality he disagrees heartily, and is always seething with temper, although he doesn't show it.

In this case, it is not nervousness, which would seem to be the obvious cause, but lack of ability. To win a good name for himself and to lose his servility, this type of salesman should study his job more, and try to improve his sales ability.

These four men, met with in most sales organisations, can all improve their position and do better, as soon as they are willing to place themselves in the appropriate category, and then use the cures outlined above.

DO YOU READ ENOUGH?

A good doctor reads his medical journals. He also keeps up to date by studying new works on medicine as they are published. The accountant reads books on accountancy; lawyers study books on law. They all know that they have to keep abreast of the times to increase their knowledge.

The salesman, however, after he has worked for a few weeks or months thinks he knows it all, when in point of fact no one ever completely masters the art of salesmanship, which should be studied continuously.

Nu-Swift, the well-known manufacturers of fire extinguishers, in their sales manual for their salesmen, print a list of books which they suggest these men should read. Some of the books cover salesmanship, others are autobiographies with inspirational value. F. Graucob, chairman and managing director of that company, went to endless trouble to see that the list was complete for his salesmen, and they, undoubtedly, benefited.

If your firm do not supply you with a similar list, visit your nearest library, compile your own list, and then start studying. A salesman should read at least one book a week dealing with salesmanship or marketing. He should also STUDY THE TRADE JOURNALS READ BY HIS CUSTOMERS.

DON'T BLOW UP

One of the qualities most valuable to a salesman is steadiness. A man who can keep steady at all times can be more useful than the up-and-down salesman.

Sales executives are given more trouble by salesmen who have been extremely successful for a short period and then have failed for a week or two, than by any other type of man.

These men are sometimes difficult to handle when they are doing well. Then comes a sticky patch. They promptly go to pieces. They blame their firm, they blame their territory, they blame their customers—they blame everyone, except themselves. Salesmen must not become too elated by success or too despondent about failure.

A good motto for salesmen is: BE STEADY AT ALL TIMES.

KEEP YOUR EYE ON THE BALL

If you are interested in golf, you will know that the same professionals top the competitions month after month, almost year after year. Over and over again, some youngster will come along and appear to be overhauling the leaders, and then he will crack. Only this morning, on looking at my paper, I noticed that one up-and-coming youngster had a first nine holes of thirty strokes. But it took him forty for the second nine.

What happened to him? At the tenth he made a mistake, sliced his drive badly, got into the rough, and it took him six strokes to get down. He couldn't forget that slice. He kept trying to correct it, but he couldn't. And so he went from bad to worse.

Every expert golfer will advise the beginner to forget all about his bad strokes, and not to be put off his play by them. It's surprising the number of salesmen who are put off their stroke by a bad interview. We have analysed many sales, and only a small percentage are conducted in an unfriendly manner. But that small percentage can do a great deal of harm—especially to the newcomer to selling.

It is quite impossible to go through your selling career without coming up against one or two buyers who are difficult to handle. One may be ill-mannered, another abrupt. If you let the bad interview live with you for the rest of the day, you won't get many orders.

When you have a bad interview spend just a few minutes after leaving the customer thinking out the cause of his rudeness. If it is something you or your company can put right, make a note of the points raised, so that you can deal with the matter later. Then forget the whole thing, and make your next call as though that interview had never taken place.

WE CAN ALL TELL THEM

It has been said, and quite rightly I believe, that the retail trade in this country could increase its turnover by as much as ten per cent if every member of the sales staff in a retail shop or store were adequately trained and supervised. There isn't a man or woman who cannot tell story after story of inadequate attention in a shop or store. Just before dictating this, I asked four members of my staff to give me their experiences of shopping during the previous week.

A. said to me, "I went into a grocer's shop and asked for a particular brand of cheese. The girl behind the counter looked up and said, 'I don't think we've got any, I'll find out'. She went away, and I saw her in conversation with another girl for three or four minutes. Naturally, I thought she was asking about the cheese. I waited patiently. When she returned she said to me, 'What was it you wanted? I've forgotten.' I walked out of the shop."

B. went into a well-known firm of gentlemen's outfitters. He wanted to buy a suit. He looked through one or two rails of suits, and the salesman said to him, "No, there's nothing there that will interest you." The salesman then did his best to persuade him to buy a suit which was more expensive than he could afford. B. again turned to the rails of the cheaper-priced suits, whereupon the salesman lost all interest in him, and gave him the feeling that if he couldn't afford to buy something good he shouldn't waste the salesman's time. He, too, walked out of the shop.

C. told of assistants standing in a group talking, and only after his direct approach to one of them did he receive any attention.

D. had little comment to make, except that he felt that when recently he bought a shirt, the assistant should not have kept up a running conversation with his manager whilst he was selling the article. He should have given his full attention to the sale.

There you have four examples of modern retail selling, but if you were to ask the retailer what he thought about the sales-man who came in to sell to him, he could tell you just as many stories. He could tell you of the 'couldn't-care-less' salesman, and the one who thought he was doing the retailer a special favour just by calling to see him.

Before you criticise others, check up on yourself.

WHAT'S YOUR SHARE?

Very few sales organisations take kindly to a new sales manager. Harry Kerr told me what happened when he first took over his job.

The directors had told him that they wanted increased sales. That was why the last sales manager had left. Kerr's job was not made any easier by the fact that many of the salesmen he was controlling had been with the company for a number of years.

Soon after he started, he sent for five of the leading salesmen to attend an informal meeting. He said to one of them who had been with the company for thirty years, "And what do you think about things? How do you think you're getting on now in view of the switch from the sellers' market to the buyers' market?"

The answer was, "Well, I get my share of the business."

Kerr turned to the next salesman. "What about you?"

The answer came, "I think that sums up my feelings, too. I think I get my share of the business, you know."

"All right, gentlemen," Kerr said, "I won't go on. But I want to put it to you this way: You men are very experienced. You know your job thoroughly; you are probably the most skilled salesmen in this particular trade in the country. Why should you be satisfied with getting your share of the business? You deserve more than your share."

Not long afterwards the men who had said that they had been satisfied with their share were already increasing their figures.

The good salesman should never be satisfied with his turnover.

RESEARCH DEPARTMENT

The majority of leading manufacturers have adequate research facilities. A research department, however, would be of little use if the managing director were not receptive to ideas.

Are you receptive to new ideas? Well, are you? You should be, and if you are you will find that new ideas will be given to you on selling and marketing, almost every week of the year.

Make a resolution right now: Never discard these ideas. Adopt this rule: Whatever idea is put to you, say to yourself, "I will try to see if it works."

The salesman's own research department can bring him rich dividends.

Old-timers, listen to this:

Recently a conference was held attended by forty leading

sales executives to discuss the question of increasing sales in a buyers' market. Now if you, reading this, happen to be a salesman of many years' experience of selling staples, I don't want you to feel annoyed at anything I am writing. I am merely recording what took place.

Each one of the sales managers present told us of the difficulties he experienced with salesmen who had been with the company a number of years, and who thought they knew everything possible about selling, were not willing to adopt any new technique, and were quite certain that at every call they made they sold everything they could sell at that call.

It's true that a salesman must build up goodwill, and do everything for his customers. But as one sales manager said, it should be fifty-fifty—fifty per cent looking after the customer, and fifty per cent for his own company. So many of these old-timers seem to work eighty per cent for their customers and twenty per cent for their company. As long as they can satisfy old Bill of Blenkinsons, with whom they have dealt for a number of years, they are quite happy even if it means taking back stock at a loss to their firm. Manager after manager told stories of salesmen who rejected suggestions for improving their selling. It seems their standard answers are always: "That's all high-pressure stuff." "That's all blah!" "That won't work with my customers." "I know my territory best."

Many instances were given of old-time salesmen retiring from a territory to be followed by another man more receptive to ideas, who actually increased business in spite of the fact that the experienced salesman had said his customers would not take kindly to any newcomer.

So, old-timer, why not admit that there's a great deal that you can still learn about selling? But don't qualify that. Having admitted it, be willing to adopt new ideas and try out new methods. Make it a rule right now that you will combine all your great experience, all the advantages you have of knowing your customers so well, with the enthusiasm of a new salesman who wants to move ahead with the times, and achieve even greater success.

Do this, and you'll lead a happier life, probably earn more

money, win the respect of your firm, and win for yourself a wonderful name—that of a greatly experienced salesman who is still willing to learn.

DEFY TRADITION

Tradition is a very good thing, but it can result in sales being lost. Too many salesmen are put off doing their jobs properly by being told that:

(a) the product cannot be sold at certain times of the year;
(b) they cannot sell in certain districts at certain times;
(c) they cannot get orders on Friday evenings;
(d) trade is only seasonal;
(e) larger firms will only see salesmen by appointment;
(f) they cannot make calls the day before a holiday;
(g) buyers place few orders during the first week of any new year; etc.

Whenever somebody tells you that you can't do this or you can't do that, always ask: "Why?"—and then don't be satisfied with the answer.

REPORTS

I remember once writing a letter to my sales manager. I can't remember the exact wording, but it went something like this:

"I can't see why you require daily reports. They don't teach you a great deal and, after all, the only thing you want from me is business. Either you trust me, or you don't. If you do, then let me carry on in my own way, and stop wasting my time filling in these daily reports."

The letter continued on those lines for about a page and a half. Since then, I must have seen hundreds and hundreds of letters from salesmen worded in a similar manner. Salesmen do loathe reports. The better the salesman, the more he hates them.

Yet I can assure you that they are essential. They keep the sales manager in touch with the work a salesman is doing, and they enable him to get guidance where necessary. Let us be frank. If everyone were a hundred per cent honest, reports would not be necessary. But the majority of salesmen don't work to a greater capacity than sixty per cent. Some reach sixty-five per cent, but it is the sales manager's job to try to increase that percentage.

A salesman is his own boss. He rarely has a supervisor with him, or anyone to watch over him; therefore the temptation to take things easy or to have an afternoon off is very great indeed. Strangely enough, most salesmen would rather not send in a report at all than write a phoney one.

A sales manager can only develop selling ideas if he knows his men's problems, and their reports do help in this direction.

Here is another sentence which I read in many letters I receive on this subject: *I get home in the evening too tired to fill in my reports.*

Most of us arrive home feeling tired, but if the man who wrote that arrived home tired and was met by a friend who asked him to have a drink or a game of billiards, he would very quickly wake up. If his hobby were cards, then he would soon forget his sleepiness when he played a game of bridge.

To kill this bogey, you should work out the exact time it takes you to fill in a report. Often you will find that it is only a matter of five or ten minutes—sometimes even two or three—which is not very long. Also, during the course of your working day you can often fill in part of the report while waiting to see a prospect.

This is how you can make your reports more interesting:

Don't look upon them as reports. Think of them as a part of your autobiography. If you do that you will find that you will derive a great deal of pleasure from keeping them up to date. Keep a copy of your reports—it's far more interesting than keeping a diary. Fill them in correctly, and in years to come you will look back upon them with interest, and you will realise that the job was well worth doing.

DON'T BE AN 'IF-ER'

A little while ago a well-known golfer said, "Give me a couple of 'if's' in a round, and I'll beat anyone."

He was referring to the average golfer's remarks—"If I'd used another club . . .", "If the ball hadn't been sliced . . .", "If the green hadn't sloped in that direction . . .", and so on.

It isn't a good thing for a salesman to become an 'if-er'. Many a man, having obtained a new job, has thought: *If only I'd taken that other job* . . . That's bad thinking. I've often heard salesmen say such things as: "If only I'd brought that sample with me to-day", and similar remarks.

This 'if-ing' business is no good, so forget about it. Forget about all the alternatives which might have meant a different job, or might have brought you another order. When you start a job, or when you start out working in the morning, decide on your line of action—and then stick to it!

BE CURIOUS

Curiosity may have killed the cat, but lack of it has often resulted in a salesman not selling as much as he should.

The good salesman should always be curious. He should want to know why things happen. He should be anxious to find out, for example, why a window display is arranged in a particular manner. The fact that certain articles have always been shown on shop counters in a certain way should not satisfy him. The salesman should want to find out why they have always been displayed like that, because he may discover ways and means of improving the layout.

He must take nothing for granted. He should be continually curious, and interested in everything. Why? Because he must have a wide knowledge, and be able to talk on practically any subject with anybody.

Henry Bowen, a crack salesman, always amazed me by his ability to do this. It didn't matter what was being discussed—

fishing, hunting, shooting, or keeping pigs, he always seemed to know something about it. The reason for this was his insatiable curiosity, which made him continually ask questions about other people's hobbies.

Here is a way in which you can check your own curiosity: You may not own or be interested in shares and the stock market, but do you study the city pages? Do you read carefully through the company reports? Do you want to know what British Industry is or is not achieving?

If you adopt the attitude that company results don't interest you—and remember, as a salesman you should know what is happening in the industrial world—then you are just not curious enough.

CHANGE YOUR MIND

Some believe that when a man has arrived at a decision he should stick to it through thick and thin. In the case of a man really expert at his job that might be the thing to do. Too many people, however, having once arrived at a decision stick to it pig-headedly, even if evidence is brought forward to prove that they are not necessarily correct in their judgment.

It is not a sign of weakness to alter your mind. All that you are, in fact, indicating is that you are wiser to-day than you were at the time your initial judgment was formed.

WATCH THAT MOLEHILL

A young salesman representing a manufacturer of refrigerators called to see me. He had been selling for about two months, after having received good training from his company.

He wanted my advice and help to find another job. I told him that he had hardly given his firm a fair chance. He answered, "It's the number of dissatisfied customers I meet. I had another case this morning. It was a service complaint, and it made me so fed up that I came along to see you, because you said I could always come to ask your help when I needed it."

I told him he had done the right thing in contacting me, but added, "Are you sure your facts are right, and that you are not making that call an excuse for either lack of confidence, lack of experience, or lack of determination on your part?"

He was most indignant about that. He said that he was very confident of himself, but he couldn't battle on against such adversity as dissatisfied customers.

"That's fair enough," I said. "Now I want you to do me a favour. I'm going to ask you to go into another office. I shall provide you with paper and pen, and I want you to write down details of every call you have made on a user since you joined the company."

"Why?" he asked.

"I'll tell you that later," I said.

Escorting him to another room, I provided him with the paper and pen, and left him. When he returned to me, I glanced through the sheet.

"Your problem," I said, "is not with your firm at all. It lies with you. You have listed here something like sixty calls on users, and only four of them were dissatisfied customers, three of whom you came across during the last two or three days. Now by the law of averages you are bound to meet dissatisfied customers, just as you are bound to meet satisfied customers. No firm in the world could hope to please everybody all the time; there is always the human factor to contend with. All sorts of things can cause a customer to be dissatisfied with a company's service—not always the company's fault, either.

"On many occasions when I have checked into service queries, I have found that the service department has done everything possible, but the customer has not been too co-operative. That doesn't mean that the firm should not do everything to satisfy him—they should. But there is no reason why that customer should break the heart of a salesman. No, what has happened to you is what happens to many new salesmen. Selling isn't easy, and you're finding it a little bit tough, so you're looking for excuses. If a salesman looks for excuses, he can always find plenty. You're with a very good firm, stick to them. Fight it out."

The young man smiled a little ruefully. "I think you're quite right, Mr. Tack," he said. "I knew that was the answer, but I was hoping that you'd say my product wasn't any good, or that with bad service I couldn't hope to succeed, and you'd tell me to get another job that is easier."

"Selling is never easy," I answered. "But you've learned a lesson. Never magnify your troubles. Never make mountains out of molehills. Whenever you are faced with difficulties of this kind, get out some facts. Don't do it by guesswork. Never use such expressions as, 'I've met dozens of people who are dissatisfied', or 'hundreds of customers complain of the quality', or 'salesmen have told me that this is a travellers' graveyard'. . . . Always work from statistics. You have written down some facts this morning which can alter your whole selling career. If you hadn't done so, you might have blamed your firm, changed your job, and have gone on failing."

MAGNIFYING TROUBLES DOES NOT HELP A SALESMAN.

MAKING FOUR EMOTIONS HELP YOU

1. *Fear*

A salesman should never be afraid to call upon a customer, however difficult that customer may be. Nor should he be afraid to call on somebody he has never seen before. If he has faith in his proposition there isn't the slightest need for him to be scared of anyone.

But here is another fear which a salesman must avoid: He should never be afraid of his fellow salesmen. He should never be scared of anyone stepping over his head. Should he become a supervisor, a manager, or a sales manager, he should never attempt to keep anyone else down, because if he is afraid of any man, that man will beat him every time. The salesman who studies his job, and works hard and conscientiously, has no need to fear anyone.

2. *Anger*

It doesn't matter much if a salesman is angry with himself for not being successful. That's the way to put things right; but it's no use being angry with your sales manager, your firm, or your customers. It is your choice to sell the proposition that you are handling. If it doesn't suit you, then change your job.

3. Dejection

When you're feeling low, then selling becomes very hard indeed. In the same way as an actor must cast off his cares as he walks on to the stage, so the salesman must forget his problems when he approaches the customer. Customers have enough worries of their own, without being depressed by salesmen. The surest way of overcoming dejection is to smile. It's very hard indeed to feel pessimistic when your face wears a smile.

4. Excitement

This is one of the finest emotions for a salesman, and it is one that he need not bother to control. Be as excited as you like about your proposition. Get excited with your selling. Get excited when you're talking to others about your job. Excitement is like enthusiasm, it's contagious. It's the finest selling emotion of all. LET YOUR EMOTIONS WORK FOR YOU, AND THEY CAN HELP YOU TO SUCCEED.

JERKS

Most books on salesmanship stress the fact that a salesman must be physically fit. Why pick on a salesman? Everyone should be physically fit. The advice to be moderate in all things is probably as good advice as any.

Many teachers of salesmanship, however, stress the fact that a salesman should indulge in physical exercises. Each morning he should stand by an open window, breathe deeply, and exercise his limbs.

Just in case you should think I am against physical training, I ought to mention that for many years I did my exercises each morning, following them with a cold bath. But I loathed that cold bath. I don't know that it made me any fitter. It certainly made me quite irritable some mornings.

If you've always been an exercise man, well then continue, it will do you the world of good. If, however, you don't like doing exercises in the morning, then my advice to you is DON'T DO THEM. They won't make you a better salesman. Of all the leading salesmen I have ever met over a number of years, I have met few who did exercises every morning.

I quite appreciate that by making this statement I am leaving myself wide open to be shot at, and that I shall, no doubt, receive a number of letters telling me of many successful salesmen who do exercises each morning. All good luck to them! I'm only giving my own experience.

Do all things *in moderation*, and you need not worry about doubling yourself up every morning.

ARE YOU A GOOD BOSS?

"The only thing Charlie knows about selling is how to sell us on the idea of working for him."

"And who is Charlie?" asked Jimmy.

"Charlie," answered Harold, "is our sales director. Likes to think he can do most of his business on the golf course, and over lunch. The times I've 'phoned him at three o'clock to find he's still at lunch!"

This is the kind of conversation you can hear any morning round about ten o'clock, in practically any coffee shop. It's a salesman's prerogative to criticise his boss—and he always uses that prerogative.

But you know the salesman's real boss is not his sales manager at all. If, instead of selling, he worked as a clerk in an office, then the office manager would be the head of his department, and would supervise his hours and his work. That doesn't apply to the salesman on the road.

It has sometimes been said that a man who acts as his own lawyer has a fool for an adviser. The salesman has to act as his own adviser and master, and it is entirely up to him whether he has a sensible person or a fool to guide him. Just remember that.

It is always up to the salesman to decide when he should start work, when he should finish, how many calls he should make, how much time he should spend on lunch, how high his own expenses should be. . . .

The salesman is his own master. He should make certain that he is a good master.

YOU DON'T KNOW YOUR OWN SELLING POWER

The managing director of a firm selling office supplies decided to organise a big competition. He had run similar competitions years earlier but in those days the cost of travel was low.

He organised a cruise to the Mediterranean. The cost worked out at about three hundred pounds a man, and the competition was open to salesmen, who could also qualify for their wives. To win, a high turnover had to be achieved for a period of three months.

Most of his executives were of the opinion that the competition was a waste of time, because they thought that no one would qualify. The average monthly turnover for his leading salesmen was about four thousand pounds a month, and these men had to step up their figures to about six thousand pounds a month to win. The competition, in spite of the pessimists, was a success. Eighteen men and their wives sailed on the cruise.

On his return, one of the leading salesmen said to the managing director, "We thought that four thousand pounds a month was about our maximum. We didn't think anybody could do better than that. But we averaged six thousand a month to qualify for that competition, so we've obviously got to set our sights a bit higher."

Since then, the turnover of these men has been well in excess of six thousand pounds a month. They did not realise their own selling power—and they were top-grade men—until they had to make extra efforts to qualify for the competition.

Many leading salesmen could sell more, if they set their sights higher.

THOSE WHO ASK GENERALLY GET

There's one sure test to find out whether a salesman is an old-timer or a new recruit. Ask him to collect cash with order, or to get a deposit. The new recruit will pale slightly, and then mutter something about firms of standing always paying monthly—asking for cash will create a wrong impression. The old-time salesman, when instructed to collect a deposit, nods his head sagely and says, "Quite right, too! No order's sound unless it's bound by a deposit. Even better will be to collect full cash with the order."

The strange thing about many business men is that they never feel that an order is binding unless they do pay a deposit. That's why cancellations sometimes take place. Even when selling staples, if a firm places a small order it is often wiser to obtain cash with order.

You can ask direct for a deposit. There's nothing wrong in doing so, but a better way is to take out a receipt book. Don't trouble to look at the prospect, but start filling it in, and then say, "By the way, sir, are you going to pay the deposit by cheque or cash?" When you put it that way, few prospects will refuse to part with their money.

TURN YOURSELF INTO A ROUND PEG

Sales executive Tom Watson always says that there need not be any square pegs in round holes. He maintains that if a man has accepted a job, he should not expect that job to line up with his requirements—he should alter himself to line up with the job.

In the main, there are five types of salesmen:

The Retail Salesman
The Staple Salesman
The Speciality Salesman
The Salesman selling Intangibles
The Sales or Technical Engineer

The Retail Salesman

The problem with most retail salesmen is that they deal with so many customers that they become tired of selling, and in fact, don't sell at all. They merely offer goods, and hope that they will be bought.

The efficient retail salesman treats every visitor to his shop as a most important customer, gives him every attention, and tries to suit his requirements. This accomplished, he is not satisfied until he is sure that he has sold his customer everything possible.

The Staple Salesman

Men with little selling experience visualise the selling of staples as being the perfect type of selling. They feel that they have only to build up a certain amount of goodwill amongst their customers to be greeted in a friendly manner on every occasion, and to get orders.

They are so keen on this friendly relationship idea that, after they have been on the road some little while, they forget to sell. They become simply goodwill workers.

Every man who sells staple goods should sell just as efficiently the hundredth time he calls on his customer as he did the first.

The Speciality Salesman

The salesman who sells specialised goods usually sells his equipment direct to user. Unless a man has perfect self-discipline, he should not become a speciality salesman. A speciality man without self-discipline is apt to take things easy on occasion, and to forget that time is all-important to him.

Speciality selling is hard. There is rarely a connection in this type of business; it means making fresh calls all the time. If you're looking for an easy way to earn a living, don't become a speciality man.

If you are looking for a very high reward, commensurate with the effort you put in, then that is the very business for you.

The Salesman selling Intangibles

The salesman selling advertising space comes under this category, he's selling an idea; also the salesman selling insurance—not the easiest form of selling, but often one of the most remunerative.

The man who wants to sell insurance should have a wide circle of friends, should have a strong personality, and should be able to sell himself so well that his clients will give him introductions which will result in more policies being sold.

The Sales or Technical Engineer

This man sells engineering products, and is usually a technical expert as well as a salesman. The problem of salesmen in this field is that they are apt to become too interested in the technical side of their business, and so forget the selling side. All men selling engineering products should make a much greater effort to study salesmanship.

Remember that even when selling technicalities a want has to be created. The buyer of such equipment is usually quite conscious of the need for it, but still that need must be turned into a want—and that can only be done *by salesmanship*.

WHATEVER JOB YOU ARE IN, OR WHATEVER SELLING JOB YOU START, FIT YOURSELF INTO THAT JOB SO THAT YOU BECOME A ROUND PEG IN A ROUND HOLE.

BUDGET

"I don't believe in cutting my expenses. I go out and earn more money."

I've heard many a salesman say that—especially when they're asking for a draw against commission.

It sounds big and worldly, but I'd far rather a man was conscious of his own earning ability, and budgeted each week to see that his expenses were not greater than his earnings.

A salesman should always fight for bigger sales and a high

income, but only the foolish salesman spends his money in advance.

Here is a good tip for the successful salesman:

Live for twelve months as you did when you first started selling. At the end of that time you won't have any more financial worries.

A salesman cannot sell properly when he is worried, so BALANCE YOUR BUDGET EACH WEEK.

WE ALL THINK WE CAN

Have you ever wanted to dash off a letter to a newspaper, because somebody is doing something that you consider inefficient, and you feel that you should write and attempt to put matters right?

Have you ever wanted to tell a garage proprietor that he doesn't know how to run his business because his garage hands are lazy or rude?

Most of us at some time or other have felt that we can run another man's business better than he can. Many salesmen think that they can run their company better than those who are in charge.

No sales executive worth his salt ever minds criticism, and he should always be willing to listen to suggestions. But suggestions can be overdone.

Here is a tip for the experienced salesman. Ask yourself this question: Although I've been with my company a long time and I'm one of the leading salesmen, *I am only a leading salesman*; they haven't made me an area manager, or given me promotion of any kind—why?

There may be many reasons, but if the reason is because you are a grouser, always telling the company's executives how to run their business, then change your methods. Don't keep writing them letters suggesting that the packing department is no good, the service department is worthless, and if you were in charge of accounts your customers would get their accounts promptly. Don't mix up suggestions with personal grouses.

Salesmen who keep grousing about their company never get far.

Make a success of your job, and let the other man do his best to make a success of his.

WILL POWER

Benny was the most nervous salesman I had ever met. The first time I saw him, he was pacing up and down outside a shop, looking so pale that I asked him if he felt all right. He answered, "No!" The trouble was, he didn't have the nerve to make a call.

Then he told me his story. His father had decided to make a man of him by removing him from his clerical job and putting him on the road—much the same idea as throwing a man into water to teach him how to swim. Benny told me that he was often sick before making a call, although that wasn't so very often, because he didn't make a great number of calls.

I have known many nervous salesmen, but none so bad as Benny. I met him a few times afterwards, and noticed that on each occasion he looked about set for the psychiatrist's couch. Then I lost touch with him for about three years.

The next time I saw him, he was sitting at the wheel of an outsize car, and appeared most prosperous.

"Hello," I said, "so you finally got out of selling." I thought that perhaps his father had died and left him a fortune.

"No," he answered. "I wouldn't give it up for anything."

"But——" I began.

"You're wondering how I got over my nervousness?" queried Benny.

"That was in my mind."

"I visited a psychiatrist——"

"Ah, I guessed——"

"Wait a minute, don't misunderstand me. His idea was that it was my imagination that was killing me. He was right, at that! I was scared of looking a fool, scared of letting the firm down, scared of everything."

"So you had yourself psycho-analysed?" I asked.

"Don't be so impatient. The doctor said that will-power

wouldn't help me because when will-power came up against imagination, the imagination would win all the time. I didn't like the idea of that, so I got off that couch and went home. Something made me want to prove that fellow wrong."

"And did you?" I said.

"Yes," he answered, "I did."

"But how?" I asked.

"Well, it's a long story," he began.

"Can't you make it short?" I said. "I have an appointment in a few minutes."

"Yes," he said, "it can be summed up pretty quickly. I was trying to do too many things too quickly. That's not the way to develop will-power. I learned the hard way that the best method of developing a strong will is not to try to be the bravest man on earth, but to tackle the small tasks first, and then go on to the bigger ones afterwards. And that is exactly what I did. For example, I telephoned some of the customers—much as I hated doing that—but at least I wasn't facing them. Soon, I began not to mind telephoning. Then I got to speaking to other salesmen. I had always been scared of that in case I looked a fool. After that, I began calling on some of the very smallest of our customers, instead of trying to get the big orders from the biggest. And so I worked my way through. . . ."

TO DEVELOP YOUR WILL-POWER, START BY TACKLING THE SMALL TASKS.

OVERSELLING

Farley was a speciality salesman, used to selling a high-priced product, and he had been successful at his job. One day he had a row with his sales manager and decided, on the spur of the moment, to leave speciality selling for selling of a different kind.

He certainly went from one extreme to the other because, through the introduction of a friend, he got a job with a firm of book publishers.

"I'll liven 'em up," said Farley. He did quite well for a time, but then one day he decided that some of his friends in the book trade were not selling as many of his books as they should.

He made a call on one of his firm's best customers, and really did enthuse over a book. He told the buyer of the quantities that other booksellers were selling, and in the end he was so persuasive that he sold him fifty copies. When he called back a month later they had only sold six copies, and that was the way Farley spoiled a splendid account for his company.

It is, of course, always the job of a salesman to increase his unit of sale. It would have been wrong for Farley to have accepted an order for three books from the bookseller, if he really felt that fifty copies could be sold. Where he made his mistake, however, was in assuming that the bookseller could do the impossible. He knew from his records that, although the book was going well, it was not going as well as all that.

Farley is now back to speciality selling, but he has learned a lesson—NEVER EXAGGERATE.

He's a better speciality salesman for learning that. When I asked him if I could print his story he said, "Yes, go ahead. I learned something from it. I hope others may as well."

Too many salesmen make exaggerated claims. Remember, it is bad to undersell, but it's much worse to make exaggerated claims.

INSULTS

How would you feel if somebody told you that you were miserly? You wouldn't like it, would you? You wouldn't be any more pleased if you were called lazy, or if a buyer inferred that you were an indifferent salesman. These are all direct insults. In my opinion, however, the biggest insult that anyone can offer to a salesman is these few words of praise:

"YOU COULD SELL REFRIGERATORS TO AN ESKIMO!"

Then, there are two other expressions which, coming from a prospect or a buyer, are insults:

"YOU ARE A FIRST-CLASS SALESMAN!"

"YOU ARE ONE OF THE BEST SALESMEN I HAVE MET!"

Has anyone ever said anything like that to you? If so, were you very pleased?

On numerous occasions, salesmen have telephoned me with joy in their voices to tell me that they have just been complimented on their salesmanship. More often than not when I have asked the salesman, "Did you get the order?" the answer has been, "No, but . . . Oh, it will come all right!"

I don't like deflating a salesman, and therefore I usually congratulate him on the order which he thinks he is going to obtain at some time in the near future. The fact is, however, that when a prospect does flatter a salesman in this way, what he is really saying is, "YOU ARE A VERY POOR SALESMAN."

Why? Because the salesman has obviously made the prospect feel that he was being high-pressured into buying. Now that can't be good selling, can it?

The first-class salesman is *the man who sells so well that a prospect doesn't realise that a sale is taking place*. When, eventually, he signs the order, he does so because he feels, after the sincere discussion which has taken place, that it will be to his benefit to buy.

It is far better to leave a prospect with the impression that you weren't a very good salesman, but with the order in your pocket, than to walk out with a praiseworthy remark that you are a crack man, but without that signed order.

The *order* is the only praise a salesman needs.

USE UP YOUR RESERVES

Carnegie once said that the reason for his success was that when he had finished a job he had no reserves. By that he meant that he put everything into the job he was doing. He didn't think of the next job, or the job after that. He did his very best with the task he was dealing with at that time.

Carnegie's advice is good for everyone. Whatever you're doing, whether it be sport or work, put everything you have into it. If you're beaten then, you'll know that there's nothing you could have pulled out which could have turned defeat into victory. But you'll find that when you work like that it isn't often that you meet defeat. Generally, you meet with victory.

THE BEST POLICY OF ALL

A. was a first-class salesman and he earned big money. It didn't last long. A. is already halfway down the hill, and is likely to slide down still farther.

B. was a brilliant salesman. Apparently, he could sell anything to anyone. He did, for a time. His position on the gradient is about the same as A's.

What was the trouble with these two men? They were both good salesmen. Why didn't they keep climbing? Why did they slide?

They were dishonest salesmen. By that I don't mean that they stole anything, or that they indulged in a sideline of smash and grab. In small ways they were dishonest to their firms.

I remember one occasion when A. was a little hard up. He had collected full cash with order, paid it into his own banking account, drawn cash against it, and sent a cheque to his firm two or three days later. The cheque was met all right. All A. had done was to find a simple way of borrowing money for a few days, without his firm's permission.

He thought he had hoodwinked his sales manager when he told him that he didn't know it was against the rules of the company. He knew the rules all right—and the sales manager knew that he knew.

B. was a similar type. He was selling equipment direct to shopkeepers. He had the habit of taking back second-hand equipment from those shopkeepers, not telling his firm about it, but selling this equipment to other dealers. Nothing really dishonest about that you might say. It didn't affect his firm. Just a little business he was doing on his own.

The whole point is, however, that he knew his firm frowned on those methods. They felt that anybody who bought a machine second-hand might be in the market for a new machine.

Now you know why A. and B. had their chances and threw them away.

It may be a little old-fashioned to say that one should strive to be honest but, all ethical reasons aside, it is a fact that from a success point of view the man who is really honest stands a far better chance than the man who indulges in get-rich-quick schemes.

HONESTY IS STILL THE FINEST INSURANCE POLICY FOR OLD AGE.

NEW YEARS' RESOLUTIONS

Don't wait until the first of the year to make a new resolution. Here's one that you can make right now—and it will help you to become successful quickly.

EVERY DAY I SHALL DO ONE THING THAT I DON'T WANT TO DO.

Yes, it's as simple as that. If you don't like making a call before nine o'clock, find someone you can call upon at half-past eight. If you don't like telephoning for appointments, then telephone for an appointment. If you don't like cutting out your morning coffee, well do without it. And so on.

Whenever something crosses your mind that you don't want to do, just go ahead, and DO IT.

WHAT'S YOUR AVERAGE?

Do you want to succeed quickly? Here's a way to do it:

DO ALL THE THINGS THE AVERAGE MAN WON'T DO.

You're not required to make that special call during a holiday period—but you make it. Someone will notice.

You always knock off at five o'clock, because that's the time of day when most shops close down? Go on looking for other businesses that keep open until six.

No one is going to pay you for overtime? Remember, executives don't get overtime pay either, and if you want to become an executive, you'll have to act like one.

It's a muddy day, so it's all right for shoes to be dirty. Is it? No, it is not! You can take a small brush with you, and polish them up before a call.

That's being above the average.

You feel that that doesn't apply to you because you've been calling on your customers for years, and they don't mind your looks? That's the way the average salesman thinks.

The average man takes old customers for granted. The able salesman makes each call an adventure, even if he is on the friendliest of terms with his buyer. He remembers that he is a SALESMAN, as well as a goodwill worker.

You can't make more than six calls a day, however hard you try? Make seven! You're not trying hard enough.

TO BE A SUCCESSFUL SALESMAN YOU MUST DO ALL THE THINGS THAT THE AVERAGE SALESMAN WON'T DO.

CHAPTER III

Fifty Ways of Closing More Orders

USUALLY, the 'Closing of the Order' is one of the last chapters in a book on salesmanship. However, until a salesman can learn how to close an order he isn't a salesman at all, he is just a conversationalist. It is for this reason that I have made 'Closing the Sale' one of my earliest chapters. I think it will also help you to get the best out of some of the chapters that follow.

EIGHT WAYS OF CLOSING AN ORDER

The good sale closes itself. This has been said over and over again. However, although a customer may be willing to place the order, he is still sometimes a little hesitant about giving his decision, and it is then that the professional salesman helps him to say yes.

We checked with a hundred speciality salesmen to see what action they took to get a 'yes', and I made the same check with a hundred men selling staple goods to retailers. Below are the results:

First, the most favoured type of close used by the speciality salesman:

74% use the Alternative close
9% use the Concession close
7% use the Summary close
3% use the Verbal Proof Story close
4% use the Fear close
1% use the Possessive close
1% use the Closing on a minor point
1% use the Ask-for-it close.

The 'Alternative' Close

This method can be used to close practically any type of sale. The 'which do you prefer' technique allows the salesman to try for a definite decision without the risk of a refusal to buy. You lose nothing by using the Alternative close. You have everything to gain. The prospect may say, "I haven't decided yet", but that will merely give you the opportunity of continuing the sale.

Use choice of colour, choice of position for installing, choice of delivery date—any alternative you can think of that is applicable to your goods. If your sales offer has been right, this close is all that you need to encourage the prospect or customer to buy.

The 'Concession' Close

The salesman who is able to grant a concession on the completion of his sales offer can often supply that extra incentive necessary to get the order. The concession can be one referring to free showcards, advertising, special circularising campaigns, delivery date, or any service you can give your customer.

The 'Summary' Close

The salesman using this close summarises all the benefits which a buyer will receive when he places his order, and then, with a smile he says, "I know you wouldn't want to be without it." He begins to fill in his order form then, assuming that an order is going to be placed.

The 'Verbal Proof Story' Close

Keep back one strong story referring to a customer who has bought your equipment and benefited considerably from the purchase. Use this final story to remove the prospect's fear of buying, and, having told it, begin to fill in the order form.

'Fear' Close

This close should be used with discretion. Many buyers react unfavourably to it, and it has antagonised many a buyer. However, on occasion it can be effective.

It can be used, for example, by a salesman selling fire extinguishers, or insurance, or by salesmen selling goods which may be in short supply later.

'Possessive' Close

This is quite a simple close. It means that the salesman implies that the customer is going to buy, long before he has arrived at any decision. A typical sentence would be, "When you have this fitted you will want it in a prominent position, won't you?"

Closing on a Minor Point

In this case the salesman avoids the main issue, but gets the customer's approval on a minor point. For example, "Do you prefer this frame?" or "Do you need extra advertising leaflets?"

'Ask-for-it' Close

This means just what it says. The salesman asks for the order, and sometimes, when all else fails, that is the best way to close. In any event, if you have tried every other method without success, always ask for the order before you leave the prospect.

Now work out ways of using each of these closes with your own product. You will then be able to use the right technique at the right time.

'STAPLE' SALESMEN

When the check was carried out with salesmen selling staples, the following were the results:

> 64% use the Write-them-down close
> 16% use the Alternative close
> 8% use the Summary close
> 6% use the Fear close
> 4% use the Concession close
> 2% use other closes.

The staple salesman finds that the best way for him to close an order is to take out his order book and begin writing in it as soon as possible. If he is unable to do this for any reason—particularly when opening a new account—then in the main, he uses the Alternative close.

SED E DANDSTA?

Do you know what that means? I shouldn't think you do. It all goes back some forty years when a small group of schoolboys had a secret society, and a secret language.

Provided I've got my basic key right, the heading means, 'Does he understand?' We used to use it when we initiated other youngsters into the society. If the new recruit didn't understand what was expected of him, he had to undergo various forms of punishment until he qualified for membership.

Well, salesmen get punished in a different way when they use the kind of language that a customer doesn't understand. No salesman, for example, should attempt to close an order until he is certain that the prospect, or customer, UNDERSTANDS EVERYTHING ABOUT HIS PROPOSITION. Orders have been closed without this understanding, but when that happens, a high percentage of them are subsequently cancelled. Usually, however, there is no order at all.

Because a salesman knows his subject himself, he sometimes fails to explain it properly, assuming that the prospect knows it equally well.

My technical knowledge is limited, and when a salesman calls to sell me something of a technical nature, if I am interested I will ask him questions. If I don't understand what he is talking about, I keep quiet—and I don't buy.

Because a prospect looks intent or interested, it doesn't mean that he is understanding all that you are telling him. It may be a pose. So here is a rule for closing:

CLOSE THE ORDER JUST AS SOON AS YOU FEEL THAT THE PROSPECT THOROUGHLY UNDERSTANDS YOUR PROPOSITION.

There is only one way of making certain that he does understand, and that is by continually asking him questions to make sure that he is following you; or by using such sentences as: "You agree with that, don't you?" or "That's right, isn't it?" or "It will do that for you, won't it?" and so on.

WORKING FOR YOUR COMPETITOR

The managing director of a company manufacturing weighing machines said to me, "The trouble with many salesmen to-day is that they are not working for their own company, they are working for their competitors. Too many salesmen do not realise that the finest opportunity they ever have of getting an order is when they first meet the buyer who is able to sign the order. Obviously, they cannot get an order on the first call if they have to tell their story to a junior member of an organisation, or if a decision depends on a committee. But in this latter case, the salesman should try to meet the committee, and that visit could then be termed his first call.

"Salesmen," he went on, "are too easily put off—*Come and see me later*—*Write me a letter*—*I'm stocked up to-day*—and all that kind of thing. But if they have been with their prospect any length of time, they have probably sold him on the idea of the equipment, and if they don't get the order themselves, then all they have done is created a sale for one of their competitors. The next man who calls could be a competitor, who will benefit from the previous salesman's sales talk, and get the order. That is what I mean when I say that too many salesmen work for their competitors."

That's right enough. During our training courses, when we have salesmen present from a wide variety of firms, some selling motor accessories, others foodstuffs, others advertising, and so on, this point is always being disputed, until we analyse the question. Then the students realise that one of the reasons why they do not close more orders is because they are weak. They would rather leave an impression of kindliness with a buyer than one of strength.

When these men have subsequently gone out on the road and made up their mind to close every possible sale on the first call, THEIR TURNOVER HAS ALWAYS INCREASED—WITHOUT UPSETTING CUSTOMERS, OR LOSING GOODWILL.

CLOSE ORDERS ON THE FIRST CALL

HOW TO CLOSE MORE FIRM ORDERS

If you close fifty sales a month, but five of the orders are subsequently cancelled, you could, obviously, increase your net sales by preventing cancellations. It always seems heartbreaking to me that an order should be cancelled when a salesman has worked so hard to make the sale. When this happens salesmen are apt to blame the buyer. They feel that he has let them down, and has acted unfairly towards them. They are wrong to do that; they should blame themselves.

Recently, I saw in a letter in a trade paper from a representative of a publishing house. After writing in a friendly way about booksellers, he went on to say that the bookseller for whom he had the least regard was the one who gave him a large order and then wrote the next day cancelling either the whole order, or a part of it. He pointed out that the bookseller would have been acting much more fairly if, at the time he placed the order, he had said that he was overstocked and he would therefore prefer to order fewer copies.

I don't blame the bookseller at all. I blame the representative. He probably showed his list, suggested quantities, wrote them down, and, because of his friendship with the buyer, obtained the order. He probably didn't sell the books, didn't explain why certain quantities should be ordered, didn't insist, for the bookseller's sake, that a large quantity of one book should be taken because of its sales potential, or a lesser number of another, because it had only a localised appeal, and so on.

The bookseller cancelled because he felt that he had made a mistake. He would not have had that feeling if the representative had sold properly. In other words, the salesmen who sell WELL get less cancellations.

YOU CAN CLOSE ON THIS

Realising the difference between two words can result in your knowing when to close an order. The two words are:

really and *want*.

Many a prospect will say to you, "I *really* ought to talk this matter over with my wife." When he says that, you will know that he doesn't need to talk it over at all. You can close.

If, on the other hand, he says, "I *want* to talk this matter over with my wife," that's a different story. Then you have to go on selling.

LOOK FOR THIS BUYING SIGNAL, AND YOU WILL KNOW WHEN TO CLOSE.

HOW ABOUT MADEIRA?

Tom Burns, before the war, sold automatic cigarette machines, and during the war he was one of the few men to sell a prison guard on the idea of helping him to escape—which he did. Since the war, his outstanding success has been in insurance.

He is a great believer in having something of a pictorial nature to help him to close the order, and he always carries with him a set of travel catalogues, including pictures of the sunny Bahamas, Madeira, and cruises to the Mediterranean. He brings these out towards the end of a sale, and says something like this:

"I'm just taking these along to the Jones's. They're very old clients of mine, and when I was there a little while ago they said they were considering going on a cruise, as they had a policy maturing." Then he goes on to say, "You know, this could happen to you in a few years' time. Nothing would give me greater pleasure than to come and see you then, and to know that I shall have helped you to take a holiday which you so richly deserve."

A good close, Tom, and one which can be applied to many businesses. Other firms' catalogues can help you to close the sale.

DON'T SPOIL THE SALE

It used to be said that there was only one psychological moment for closing a sale, and if that was missed no order would result.

That theory was disproved many years ago, and nobody now thinks on those lines. But this I do believe—although there may not be a psychological moment for closing an order, there is definitely a psychological moment for spoiling an order. A good salesman knows when this happens. All is going well, when suddenly there is a change of manner on the part of the buyer. It happens so quickly, too. At one moment the prospect is bubbling over with enthusiasm, and the next it has all gone. What is the cause?

Usually, the cause is the salesman talking too much, and for too long. The prospect switches from interest to boredom, and that's that.

LOOK TO THE FUTURE

A well-known insurance salesman, John Slade, told me of this close:

He tells the prospect the story of a neighbour of his who had once been a successful business man, but had lost his money through ill-health, and had to live with one of his children. The old gentleman, he explains, is so shabby that he won't go out during the daytime.

This often irritates the prospect, until John says, "You know, Victor Hugo had it right when he said, '*Nothing, not even prison bars, can hold a man as securely as can poverty in old age*'."

Slade said that that quotation has brought him many, many sales.

PAINTING A PICTURE OF THE FUTURE CAN HELP ALL SALESMEN TO CLOSE MORE ORDERS.

'TRY-OUT' CLOSES

On many occasions a salesman, thinking that the right moment has arrived, asks for the order, receives a refusal, and is so shaken by this that he hardly has any fight left in him. The extraordinary thing about prospects is that often those who appear to be most interested are the very people who won't sign the order in the end.

Every salesman should continually use try-out closes to discover what headway he is making. The salesman selling an article which requires special fixing can put it this way:

"You mentioned, sir, that you're a very good carpenter and handyman. Is this the sort of thing that you could fix yourself, or would you employ your builder?"

That's a typical try-out close. If the prospect answers, "I think it might be a little too difficult for me", or "I could do that all right, but I don't think I have the time", or "Yes, I could put that up easily enough", you'll know that you're getting very well on the way towards the order.

These trial closes must never be so worded as to bring a negative reply. If the reply shows that the prospect is still uncertain, you can see that you're not making as much headway as you should, and you must fight a little harder. But if you get a positive reply, you do, indeed, know that you are very near the sale.

FIVE WAYS OF CLOSING A SALE

1. Early in the sale try to close the order (or part of the order) by using such a sentence as, "Will you need six, or will three be enough?" or "Will you be able to wait three weeks for delivery, or would you like us to rush the order through?"

   This kind of sentence may bring a negative reply, but it will not mean that you won't get the order, and it might help you to close the sale with the least possible delay.

2. Use your pen as much as you can during the sale. Use it for working out profit figures, or to prove a sales point. Do this, because it will allow you to let the prospect use your pen to work out his own figures. When the time comes for you to close the sale, it will be easier if the prospect has your pen in his hand.

3. When you have finished a sales sequence, try to tell an interesting story. This takes the prospect's mind off his mental conflict as to whether or not he should buy. When you have finished your story, use the Alternative close, and the prospect will more often than not sign the order form.

4. From the beginning of a sale, always assume that you are going to get the order.

5. Remember, a salesman is not a salesman until he can close an order. When a prospect says no, that is when the professional salesman really starts to fight.

THE 'SALES AID' CLOSE

It was a hot and steamy night; the humidity seemed to be about one hundred per cent. All around me were men and women perspiring freely, and the conditions were anything but right for a pleasant evening—and yet we did have a pleasant evening.

It was in 1948, and we were watching Joe Louis defend his title against Jersey Joe Walcott. There wasn't much excitement to start with, the men looked like two black marble statues after a cleaner had poured water over them, and the lighting above the ring reflected from their shining bodies.

Louis shuffled after Walcott, hardly hitting at all, but moving forward all the time. Walcott boxed on the retreat, but he kept slipping under Louis' arms and scoring with his left. Louis hardly used his right at all—he kept it back for the pay-off. And the pay-off came. Unexpectedly that right came across, and when it landed we all knew that Walcott wouldn't recover

—and he didn't. Joe Louis never wasted his right—HE KEPT IT BACK FOR USE AT THE RIGHT MOMENT.

Too many salesmen waste their best punches early in the sales battle. Because they are armed with a host of sales aids and a string of verbal proof stories, they feel it is their duty to show everything, and tell everything, as quickly as possible. They haven't the time to show pride of ownership in their leaflets. They produce them so quickly that any startling effect which they should have on the prospect is lost.

This is brought about by the salesman's anxiety to impress quickly, and to overwhelm the prospect with his sales aids and talk. Enthusiastic selling is always good, provided the salesman knows what he is doing and is not just losing his head. The element of surprise is as important in a sale as it is in a fight.

Most salesmen have one particular sales aid which they prefer to all others. All salesmen have one story which they like to tell, because it always gets a good reaction. Now here's my advice to you:

RETAIN IN YOUR BAG WHATEVER YOU CONSIDER TO BE YOUR BEST SALES AID UNTIL THE SALE IS AT LEAST THREE-QUARTERS OF THE WAY THROUGH.

And at the same time, KEEP YOUR BEST STORY FOR USE AS A CLOSING AID.

Now take time off to think about this, and when you have decided on your sales aid, then put it aside, and keep it back as long as you can. Every time you are tempted to use it during a sale—wait a little longer.

This will result in your sales story being better, because you are building it, to start off with, around your weaker tools. It means that you will have to rely more on your sales ability. Then, when you bring out your best ammunition, you will find closing the order will become much easier for you.

The rule for every salesman to remember is to USE HIS SECOND BEST SALES AID FOR THE APPROACH, AND HIS BEST SALES AID FOR THE CLOSE.

THE FINAL CLOSE

As a younger man, one of the most nerve-racking experiences I ever had was working under a supervisor who was more than slightly deaf.

Carrying on a normal conversation with him wasn't easy, but to be with him while a sale was taking place was sheer embarrassment.

He never seemed to hear the objections of the prospect. He went blithely on with his sales talk. At the end of every sale, whether he had been met with blank refusal or not, he would produce his order form and ask for the order—this sometimes when prospects had been almost rude to him, telling him that he was wasting their time. Invariably he asked. And the amazing thing is that quite a fair proportion of those prospects who had been most emphatic with their noes did buy something when asked for the order.

This is so hard to believe that if I hadn't taken part in those sales myself I couldn't believe it. But it did happen. Often, after such sales had taken place, I would say to him, "But how could you ask for the order, in view of what he had been telling you?"

He would just smile and say, "Well, I didn't hear him say much about it. I thought he was quite interested."

I often wondered if he really was as deaf as he made himself out to be. However, he taught me a great lesson, and that was: *Ask for the order at every call.* It doesn't matter how hopeless the call may seem, ask for the order. A percentage will buy, and that percentage will amply repay you for any embarrassment you may feel at the look of surprise on the face of some prospects when, after they have been saying "no" for so long, you ask them to sign the order.

BENEFITS CLOSE ORDERS

There can be half a dozen different opportunities during a sale for closing the order. Sometimes it is possible to close an order very much earlier, just by asking for it. But this risk is not worth while. It's the same as trying to use a wood in the rough at golf. It may come off once in a hundred times, but the other ninety-nine will cost you quite a few strokes.

When you try to close an order quickly, you do so because you feel that the prospect has reacted favourably to your sales story. Often, however, the buyer who appears to be enthusiastic is just a natural enthusiast about everything. That doesn't mean that he is ready to place his order every time he looks pleased with what you have told him. If there were anything in this, then the miserable-looking buyer would never be asked for the order at all.

It is only when you feel satisfied that you have explained ALL THE BENEFITS YOUR PRODUCT WILL BRING TO THE PROSPECT that you should feel entitled to close that order.

YOU CAN'T LOSE AN ORDER

When Johnson called at my office to see me, I quickly noticed that he was not in the most pleasant of moods. In fact, he was all burned up. He gabbled away, fifteen to the dozen, about the trials and tribulations of selling, and most of all his temper was directed towards wives in general, and one wife in particular. He finished up by saying, "I was certain of that order. I knew I was going to get it, it was in the bag. Then, because she interfered, I lost it."

"Do you possess a music centre?" I asked him.

He answered, "No!" and looked quite surprised at my question.

"I couldn't very well steal it from you then, could I?" I went on.

"Steal what? I told you I haven't got one!"

"That's what I mean," I said. "You couldn't have come into my office this morning and bemoaned your fate because you had lost your music centre, because you don't possess one."

"What are you getting at, Mr. Tack?"

"Just this," I said. "Too many salesmen talk about losing

orders. No sale ever was lost—you can't lose something you don't possess. You never had the order that you've been telling me about, so why are you getting all worked up? If you'd had the order form signed and handed to you, and then subsequently the wife had torn it up, you could say that you had lost the order. Too many salesmen," I went on, "only *think* they have an order, and then they are most upset when the order form isn't signed.

"There is only one reason why that woman interfered, and why you, in fact, didn't get the order, and that was because you hadn't sold well enough. There is no other reason whatsoever! You can't blame the wife—she didn't take anything away from you. You didn't sell well enough to get her consent in the first place. She didn't alter her mind, and she didn't alter her husband's mind. If she had been properly sold you wouldn't be in my office now."

Johnson looked a little uncomfortable, so I said, "Don't worry, everyone who has sold has felt, at some time, as you feel now. But you can only profit from feeling so irritable if you are willing to realise that when a sale is not made it is not the fault of the prospect—it is the fault of the salesman.

"There is one way," I said, "in which you can be more certain of knowing whether, in fact, you do lose an order, as you put it, and that is by getting the order form made out. Many sales are lost because of that last-minute attempt to close. It is at this stage that a wife, or partner, interferes.

"The most certain way in which you can find out how you are progressing with your sale is to produce your order form as early as you can, and start writing it. When you do this, and you get a bad reaction from the prospect, you will know that you are not making a good sale, and you've got to sell all the harder. If, on the other hand, the prospect, his wife, or partner or anyone else in the shop doesn't seem to mind you writing on the order form, then you have received the finest of all buying signals. So, Mr. Johnson," I said finally, "forget once and for all about losing_orders. Think in a more positive way of how to gain orders—and the most positive method is the assumption that you are going to get the sale, so that it is right for you to produce the order form early, and to start making notes on it.

"When you sell in that manner," I went on, "you will find out that eventually your prospect will buy from you, and there will be less talk about these so-called lost sales."

THE CLOSING TREBLE

Too many salesmen stop themselves from getting orders by making foolish mistakes when the time comes for the prospect to sign. Here are the points you must watch carefully:

1. Remember that it is only fear which is stopping him from buying. He is afraid that he may lose money; he is afraid that he may be overspending; he is afraid of what his wife will say; he is afraid of what his managing director will say.

   The only way to alleviate his fears is to reassure him. So when you get near to the close, tell him again, *in a positive manner*, of the benefits he will receive from placing his order with you. Tell him how pleased his wife will be, or his managing director. Point out again how he will be saving money, or make more profit.

2. The one certain way of stopping yourself from getting the order is to be negative in your sales talk when the close draws near—"Yes, I think it will do that", "I think that will be all right".

   CUT OUT ALL NEGATIVE EXPRESSIONS and tell the prospect *positively* that he is doing the right thing by placing an order.

3. DON'T ANNOY THE PROSPECT AT THE LAST MINUTE. Many salesmen irritate the prospect by doing silly little things—perhaps making a feeble joke—an odd, tactless remark—strewing a lot of papers over his counter, thus hiding his showcase from his customers. . . .

When the time comes to close, in a quiet but firm manner ask for an order number, or for a signature on your own order form.

FOURTEEN WAYS OF CLOSING MORE ORDERS

As a salesman has to fight for his order on many occasions, it will pay him to remember the formula of the seven noes. This formula is quite simple—it applies mainly to the speciality salesman.

He must be prepared to take no less than seven "noes" from a prospect before he gives up the battle.

On hundreds and hundreds of occasions salesmen have closed orders after the second or third "no". It is a fact, however, that many salesmen do not obtain the orders they should, because they are not aware that the prospect is ready to buy.

I believe that there can be half a dozen occasions during a sale when the order can be closed, and each of these occasions has arisen because the salesman has made the prospect want his goods, and the prospect is ready to buy. Many salesmen, however, lose the opportunity by not realising that the order can be obtained at that point. Some men have a natural intuition which tells them when the best moment for closing has arrived, but you haven't got to worry about intuition. All you have to be concerned with is your sight and hearing. Make use of these two senses, and you will close many more orders.

When the prospect glances through your order form, he is ready to buy.

When the prospect picks up a leaflet which he has previously studied and starts to read it again, he is ready to buy.

When a salesman is selling staple goods he has only to watch the customer, and when that customer picks up a sample again and looks at it, or glances round his shelves as if checking up on his stock, or talks about delivery, or queries whether showcards are supplied, he is ready to buy.

When the prospect wants to show a leaflet or a sample to a colleague, he is ready to buy.

When the prospect agrees with you, perhaps saying, " Yes, the equipment is well designed", he is ready to buy.

When a prospect asks, "Will it help me do this, or that?" he is ready to buy.

When a prospect asks questions regarding spare parts or service, he is ready to buy.

You will see, therefore, that during a sale there can be many, many occasions when you can obtain an order.

If a salesman is unobservant, too concerned with himself, too concerned with his own story, too oblivious of what is going on around him, he will lose dozens of sales; he will fail to obtain many orders because of his inability to realise that he only has to ask for the order to get it.

To improve your closing technique, watch for the buying signals. The first time you see or hear one, then quietly, but firmly, ASK FOR THE ORDER.

THE 'CANCELLED ORDER' CLOSE

Henry Dobson sells fire extinguishers. He told me of a close he uses. He didn't like telling me at first, because he said that he had originated it, and he didn't see why he should teach it to others. This, of course, intrigued me, so I persuaded him to tell me about it, and finally got him to agree to let me print his story.

"This is the way I do it," he said. "When I can't get the order any other way, I take out my order form and fill it in. The prospect invariably asks 'What are you doing?' or 'What's that for?' I don't answer. When it is completed I say to the prospect, 'Would you mind writing cancelled across this order form, and initialling it?' Usually he says, 'But why do you want me to do that?'

"I answer, 'Well you see, sir, I keep these cancelled orders. I have quite a few of them in my bag here. Every year there are thousands of fires. Obviously, a great many of them occur in business premises not equipped with fire extinguishers. Some of them are firms I've called upon, who wouldn't buy from me. My firm try to keep a record of fires, and they check up and want to know why a salesman hasn't called. So if you'll just initial this—well, of course, I hope it won't happen, but if you should have a fire and the place burns down, at least my firm will know that I've done my duty. They will know that I have been to see you, to try to give you the protection you need."

Henry told me that that close works fifty per cent of the time. With the other fifty per cent he finds his normal closes are effective.

NO MAN LIKES TO PUT INTO WRITING THAT HIS JUDGMENT MAY BE WRONG.

THE 'REFUSAL' CLOSE

Strip cartoons are now a part of our daily existence. I saw quite a good one in the *Daily Express*, where the adventures of the Gambol Family are recorded.

Mr. and Mrs. Gambol visit a store together—Mrs. Gambol wants to buy a dress. She sees the very dress she wants, but at the same time another customer spies it and the two women begin squabbling about who should have it.

Mr. Gambol then calls the assistant aside and begs her to see if she can find another dress, to stop the argument. As a special favour the assistant goes into the stockroom and finds another dress of the same make and design.

"Here," says Gambol, when the assistant returns, "the problem is solved. Now you can both have the same kind of dress."

As soon as the women see that there are two dresses alike they both refuse to buy, and walk out of the shop in opposite directions.

The point of this is that many people are most anxious to buy when they are not allowed to buy—when they are told that they should not have something, or they cannot have something. A salesman who sells ladies' dresses told me that on practically every call he makes he has in mind a couple of dresses that he's not going to allow the buyer to have if he can possibly help it. On looking through the range he will say to the buyer, "No, I shouldn't have that one", "I don't think that is the type of dress you'll sell in this store", "It isn't good enough for your trade", or something like that.

He explained to me that not only is this a tremendous confidence builder but, human nature being what it is, these very models are sometimes purchased against his advice.

Generally speaking, however, it is best to use this angle as a close. When the time comes for the order form to be filled in, it is a good thing for the salesman to say, "I shouldn't have that", or "Don't buy too many of those"—the assumption being that the buyer is going to place an order for his other samples.

You can sometimes close by refusing to sell.

THE 'GETTING APPROVAL' CLOSE

Here is a good way of closing the order when the prospect is dubious. Ask for his opinion. For example: "What do you think of this plan?" or "What do you think of this display card? We send it with the goods", or "What do you think of this method of installation?", or "What do you think of our special delivery by instalment plan?"

This will often start the prospect talking, and in many cases he will talk himself into buying—which, after all, is far better than the salesman having to close the order on a strong selling point.

THE 'MAKE A DECISION' CLOSE

The bugbear of all salesmen is the sentence: "I want to think it over." Here is a way to overcome this:

"You know, sir, we've been through everything point by point, and you've agreed with our plan. So what is there to think about? There's one thing I'm certain of—indecision is not one of your weaknesses. You wouldn't be as successful as you are to-day if you were not the type of man who can make up his mind on the spot."

TELL A MAN THAT HE IS A MAN OF DECISION AND OFTEN HE WILL BECOME ONE.

THE 'SPECIAL TERMS' CLOSE

Many salesmen sell products which are offered for cash, or on hire purchase or deferred payments. Payments may possibly be spread over six, nine, twelve months, or more. Here is a good close for salesmen selling on terms when the prospect says, "I can't afford it."

"I appreciate that," answers the salesman, "but look, sir, I'd like to ask you this question: Could you save a penny a month?"

The prospect will invariably answer, "Well, of course, I could."

"All right, sir," says the salesman, "could you save a hundred pounds a month?"

The prospect shakes his head. "No," he says, "I couldn't do that."

"Very well, then," says the salesman, "we've proved one thing—that somewhere between a penny a month and a hundred pounds a month is an amount that you could save. Now all we have to do is to find that amount and we can still do business."

The salesman then works out with the prospect how much he can afford to take out of his business each month to pay for the equipment, and signs him up on those terms—provided the amount is within the range of the terms he can offer.

SAVE YOUR HIRE PURCHASE TERMS FOR THE CLOSE.

THE 'PICK UP THE CASE' CLOSE

It is most difficult to sell to a prospect who is taut and tense. The right time to push home any advantage is when he is relaxed. Even if you can make him relax temporarily it can result in a swing in your favour.

When you have tried everything else to close the order and you have not succeeded, here is something more you can do.

PICK UP YOUR CASE.

This act is so final that the prospect always feels that you are finished, and are about to leave. In most cases he then does relax. As you move away, turn and make one more attempt to close the order.

I have seen that close work time and time again. The reason why it works is that we can never read the other man's mind, and we never know how near we are to getting the order. Possibly, while the prospect is saying, "No, not to-day, thank you", he is really thinking that he might give you an order. He is hoping you'll go, but half hoping that you'll stay.

If you pick up your case he will sigh with relief. You will have made up his mind for him. Then turn, put your case down again, and make one more attack. More often than not then he will give way.

REMEMBER, A CASE PACKED WITH AN AIR OF FINALITY CAN HELP TO CLOSE THE ORDER.

CLOSE FROM THE APPROACH

Smith was the first salesman I ever employed. I had started up in business on my own—selling fancy goods. I felt that I couldn't really call myself a successful business man running a large organisation unless I had some staff. I typed my own letters, and dealt with my own correspondence. I couldn't afford anyone to do the office work. I packed my own parcels, and delivered the goods myself. But I did want to employ someone, so one day I hit upon the idea of employing a salesman. I thought that shouldn't cost me anything. So I employed Smith.

He wasn't a first-class man, otherwise he wouldn't have joined me. I made it clear to him that although I should pay him a wage, if at the end of the first week he had not sold enough to cover his wages, we should have to part company. That didn't encourage him much.

We divided the West End territory. I said I would deal with one half and he could look after the other. I would then go back to the office and see to the packing and despatch, while he went out into the suburbs.

On Tuesday afternoon he came into the office. He had hardly

booked an order. "The trouble is," he said, "that I don't seem to be able to close the order. I show all the samples. I think they're interested. I think I'm going to get a sale. And then when I've finished showing them, the buyer says, 'Thank you very much, but there's nothing I really want at the moment. Come and see me again next week.' Do you think I'm doing anything wrong?"

Then I had a brainwave, and I've remembered it ever since. I didn't know anything then about sales talk or sales sequences, but for all that I had already had a good experience of selling, so I said, "I'll tell you when to close the order—just as soon as you've made the approach."

"I don't understand you," answered Smith.

"It's clear enough. *You* show all your samples, wait till the end, and then hope that you'll get the order. You come with me right now, and I'll show you what I mean."

Out of the office we went and we called on a small fancy goods shop just off Knightsbridge. I made the usual approach, opened my case and produced my first sample—it was a novelty stamp licker. It was made in the shape of a dog, and when its tail was moved it put out its tongue and the stamp could be moistened.

"Yes," said the buyer, without comment as I showed it to her, waiting for me to show the next sample.

But I didn't show her anything else. I said, "I'll book you six of these, shall I?"

Rather to my amazement—and certainly to Smith's, she said, "Not six, I'll have three to start with."

Then I went on showing other goods in the range. I didn't get an order for each sample shown, but I did get quite a nice order

When we left the shop I said, "See what I mean? A salesman should think of the close as soon as he makes his approach."

THE RIGHT WAY TO CLOSE AN ORDER

There is only one easy way to close an order, and that is to MAKE YOUR SALES STORY SO PERFECT THAT THE ORDER WILL CLOSE ITSELF.

CHAPTER IV

A Hundred Proved Ways of Getting the Most Out of a Territory

MOST sales managers if given the choice of engaging a sales-man of average ability who would work in the right way, or a salesman with exceptional ability who would not give much thought to the way he worked, would choose the man in the first category. The ideal, of course, is for a man to be a first-class salesman, and to work in the proper manner. This is something which you will want to achieve.

THE BEST PLAN OF ALL

Hundreds of firms, and hundreds of salesmen, have tried to find some short cut whereby they can, without a great deal of physical effort, contact the greatest number of prospects or customers each day. Every salesman knows that the only time that is of value to him is the time he spends with a customer or prospect. Statistics prove that the great majority of salesmen never work to more than sixty per cent capacity.

Many salesmen are able to telephone customers/clients/prospects to obtain interviews. This does cut down time wasted in travelling perhaps a long way to be met with, "Mr. Smith is out". Telephoning for appointments needs special skills without which a salesman can waste more time on the telephone than by making the calls, even if some are abortive. Sometimes salesmen use telephoning as an excuse to stay at home all day rather than to go out on a cold, showery, wintery day. Most salesmen, while using the telephone occasionally, will, in the main, contact the majority of customers/clients/prospects by calling directly on them.

Whether selling by telephone, making appointments for interviews by telephone, or calling regularly on customers/ clients/prospects, there is only one way to work: systematically.

Work Systematically

Working systematically is the great time saver. Men selling staple goods feel that this does not apply to them, but it is just as applicable in their case as it is to speciality salesmen. Most businesses lose fifteen per cent of their customers every year. This can happen because of a change of buyer, the death of a customer, or by customers feeling that they can buy better elsewhere. It is the duty of the staple salesman, therefore, not only to call systematically, but to keep on the lookout all the time for new outlets for his goods.

Here is the only satisfactory way to work a territory:

(a) If you are a speciality salesman able to sell to every type of trade, then cold canvass your area, shop by shop, street by street.

(b) If you sell only to factories, then find out details of every factory in your area, and call upon them one after the other, systematically.

(c) If you call on architects, doctors, local authorities, be sure to call in a logical time-saving sequence.

Enquiries

I am sometimes asked what method should be adopted if a salesman has to deal with enquiries. One firm I know doubled its turnover by the simple expedient of limiting its salesmen to one enquiry each a day. Before they did this, salesmen were dealing with enquiries covering a wide area, and spending nearly all their time travelling. Now they are taught to try to make an appointment with the buyer making the enquiry as late in the day as possible. They are then told to get to that part of the territory by nine in the morning, and to work it systematically before dealing with the enquiry.

Wasted Time

Sometimes a salesman has an hour to spare before keeping an appointment, but is afraid of making another call in case it makes him late. He should not waste the time, however. If possible, he should make calls and perhaps deal with one item in his range only, so that he will not take up too much time in selling. On other occasions, he can spend the time trying to find new outlets for his goods.

Car or Foot

Sometimes it can be a big disadvantage to use a car, especially in a town. A salesman is so apt to drive past likely users because of parking difficulties. If you possibly can, you should work on foot in town rather than by car.

Work Systematically

There is no alternative to working systematically. It is the only certain way to achieve success. The more time you spend in trains, buses or cars, the less money you will earn. Whatever your sales ability may be, you can add to your turnover and income if, every day of the week, you remember to work systematically.

THE GRAVEYARD

At our personal training courses I ask the students to choose any letter they like from a file of letters which I have available during my lecture on 'How to Work'. These letters have been sent to the sales managers of various companies, and were written by salesmen working every county in the British Isles. The letters which are chosen are then read aloud.

In each of them there is a phrase which reads something like this:

> *Of course, this area is known throughout the selling world as the travellers' graveyard!*

Of all the myths in the selling world which need exploding that is the one which should go sky high, and the production of these letters usually has the right effect.

There are letters from Lancashire salesmen complaining about the state of the cotton industry; letters from men in the Midlands worried about unemployment in the car industry; an Eastern counties representative calls his territory the graveyard because the people there are so insular that they don't take easily to anything new; a salesman in Glasgow complains bitterly that his territory is a graveyard for English salesmen because the buyers are clannish; a representative from Bristol is certain that his territory is the worst because Bristolians take such a long time to make up their mind about anything; in South Wales a representative complains that his territory is finished because a tinplate factory has just closed down. . . .

None of these letters is original in its wording, because all of them contain this sentence: 'I know you won't believe that my territory is different, but it is different because . . .' In other words, the salesman is trying to make it clear that all other salesmen's complaints are not valid, although his is.

This is nothing new. It has been going on for years. As soon as a salesman's figures drop he thinks he has the worst possible territory.

There are problems in every territory, but there are sales to be made in every territory. So next time you want to blame your ground just think of all the letters we have here, and remember that thousands of salesmen believe that they are right and you are wrong, because many of them would like to have the opportunity of working your territory in the same way as you feel that you might like to work their areas.

Make one resolution right now: *never again complain about your territory*. There are no bad or good territories—only bad or good salesmen.

THINK THIS OVER

Two sales directors called to see me. The first began his selling career during a recession—plus having to compete against imported goods undercutting prices. He knew what really tough selling meant.

He said, "I well remember when first I came to London as a salesman to work with my company. I was greeted by an old-timer who said to me, 'It's no use trying to sell our stuff before ten-thirty in the morning. You won't find many works managers or managing directors who will see you before then.' Luckily, I did not take his advice. I soon found that there were plenty of works managers and directors who were willing to see me at eight-thirty and nine o'clock in the morning."

That man is now the sales manager of his company. I wonder what happened to the old-timer who gave him that advice!

The next executive I talked to asked me, "What can I do to get my salesmen to make better use of their working time?"

"To begin with," I said, "ask them for time reports, and make certain that the salesmen don't think their starting time for work is the time they leave home. The starting time for work is when they make their first call."

At this he said, "Well, I hardly like to admit it, but one of my salesmen, who lives outside his area and has an hour's journey, leaves his home at nine o'clock each morning, and he couldn't, therefore, make his first call before ten, at the earliest."

"Just think of that alone!" I said. "Five hours a week thrown away. Two hundred and fifty hours a year wasted."

After we had parted I was beginning to feel proud of myself and the advice I had given him, when my secretary rang through to say that Mr. X. had called to see me. Mr. X. was one of my own salesmen. Obviously, I thought, the visit must be of extreme importance. I saw him immediately.

He had travelled something like nine miles through London traffic, which must have taken him a full hour, to ask me to settle a query which I could have dealt with over the telephone in about thirty seconds. It referred to an inquiry which he had received from another territory, and he said that he didn't know what he should do about it.

I wasn't nearly so proud of myself when that man left me, *because he had wasted at least two hours of valuable working time.*

This, then, is a major problem. It is a problem which, if it could be solved, would result in practically every company increasing its turnover by anything from ten per cent to thirty per cent. Just imagine that!

Think it over carefully, and make up your mind that from now on you will make your first call by not later than nine o'clock in the morning, and your last call by not earlier than five-thirty; that during the day you will not waste time by useless calls, by idle chatter, by yarning over coffee, or by spending too much time over lunch. The future comes all too quickly. Think of the one man who became an executive, and the other who has probably failed.

MAKE UP YOUR MIND, RIGHT NOW, THAT THAT KIND OF THING WILL NEVER HAPPEN TO YOU, BECAUSE YOU HAVE LEARNED THIS MOST VALUABLE LESSON IN SELLING—TIME IS MONEY TO A SALESMAN.

NINE POINTS TO HELP YOUR BUSINESS

It is said of Patterson, founder of the National Cash Register Company, and originator of many of the selling ideas used to-day, that he once promoted a man from the position of salesman to sales manager because in answer to the question, "Why do you like working for me?" he said, "Because you put me in business for myself. You have given me a territory, you have provided me with the goods, and you lay out all the cash. This is far more than the average man who starts in business for himself can hope to obtain."

The salesman should always think that way—that he is in business on his own account. He should look upon his territory as his shop, his office, his domain. It is a good thing on occasion for a salesman to work out the value of his territory, and he should do it in this way:

1. Map out the exact extent of the territory and outline it on the map.
2. Find out its population.
3. Calculate the number of potential buyers on that territory.

4. List the names of users of his products, and, when doing this, ask for his firm's help. Sometimes a firm loses touch with some of its old users, but they are worth looking up.

5. Note the amount of business that the territory is producing.

6. Estimate the total volume of business the territory could produce.

7. Try to assess the amount of business his competitors are getting.

8. Try to find out why his competitors are getting that business, and how much of it he could take from them.

9. Always have a record of any special festivities or activities which take place on his territory from time to time, so that he can link-up the sale of his own good with these gala occasions.

BUYERS, AND HOW TO SEE THEM

The newcomer to selling is often worried as to how he can gain admission to the buyer, and the kind of reception he will receive when he does see him. The old-timer knows most of the angles, but even he can sometimes be sidetracked. This is the way it usually works out:

Calling on Shops

The salesman who calls regularly on shopkeepers has no problem. In nearly every case the owner of the shop does his own buying, and is quite willing to see anyone who can interest him in something that can benefit his business.

Selling Insurance

The salesman selling life insurance often finds it extremely hard to get past the commissionaire or receptionist, and although he must make a high percentage of his calls from cold, his best method of meeting new people is to work up a recommendation list. No insurance salesman can succeed unless he can sell himself so well to his clients that they are willing to pass on to him the names of their friends who might be interested in insurance.

No need to use the name of the client who gave the recommendation in cases where they wish to remain anonymous. The information given to the salesman about the new prospect will enable him to get an appointment by telephone, or to get an interview by a direct call.

Every salesman has heard of the expression *make use of your users*. The salesman selling insurance cannot remember this too often.

Selling to Industry

Under this heading I would include the head offices of large companies, in which the executives are often guarded by commissionaires or receptionists. In the first place, the salesman must find out the name of the person he wishes to see. Many firms have buying offices, in charge of which are buyers. Salesmen should not be misled by the name. In the majority of cases the buyer does not buy at all, he merely countersigns orders, or obtains quotations for goods needed at the factory.

When selling to industry, the salesman must discover the person responsible for buying his goods. If it is stationery, may be the office manager or general manager. Possibly the welfare officer will handle certain equipment. The canteen purchases may be dealt with by a canteen manager; the works manager will buy machinery, and so on. My advice to all salesmen, however, when selling capital equipment, is always to try to see the managing director. Except for a few large public companies, the majority of firms do not buy capital equipment unless the managing director sanctions the purchase. The salesman is often told that the matter has to go before the board of directors, but more often than not the only man who counts on that board of directors is the managing director.

There is, however, the snag of getting past the receptionist. Sometimes it is as well to telephone for an appointment, but it is so easy for a managing director to be negative over the telephone. Some salesmen are able to write and obtain an appointment by letter, but this rarely happens to the salesman selling specialised products. Directors receive so many letters asking for appointments, and they are interested in so few. Here is the proof: If a company indulges in a circularising campaign and offers to send further information on receipt of a pre-paid card, they are very lucky if they receive replies amounting to two per cent. The average is about one and a half per cent. But if a similar circular were sent with the object of getting an appointment for a representative, then the response would drop to something like one reply in a thousand letters. I am excluding, of course, special offers of bargain goods.

Letters in the main, then, do not get appointments.

The advice given by nearly every sales executive to salesmen selling specialised products who come up against the receptionist snag, is not to use a card. Leaving a card is useless for a speciality salesman. It will generally find its way into the waste-paper basket.

A good approach to a receptionist is: "Good morning, will you tell Mr. Higginbottom that Mr. Jones is here." As soon as he says this the salesman should move away. He should not invite further questioning.

The receptionist will usually then ring through to the managing director and give Mr. Jones' name, when the chances are about even that he will be seen. But even if the odds were worse than that, they would still be better than using a visiting card.

George Drexler, Chairman and Managing Director of Ofrex, the well-known suppliers of office stationery and equipment, told me that he always used that approach when he first started his company. He elaborated slightly by spelling his name slowly. He would say, "Tell Mr. Higginbottom that Drexler is here to see him—D-r-e-x-l-e-r—Drexler. Right?" The fact that he spelt his name slowly to the receptionist seemed to convey to her that he was someone of importance, and he wanted to make certain that she conveyed his name correctly to the managing director.

Using this approach enabled him to sell to the chief executives in some of our largest industrial organisations.

HE'S BUSY

"What should I do when the buyer is busy?" That is a question I am often asked, particularly by young salesmen. Usually they are referring to the shopkeeper who is serving customers when they call. The rules are quite simple:

(a) If the shopkeeper is busy and you feel that he will be free quickly, then wait outside the shop. Don't wait inside the shop unless there is plenty of room for you.

(b) If it looks as though the shopkeeper is going to be busy for any length of time, try to make some calls elsewhere. Every minute you spend queueing up is money lost for you.

(c) If, after waiting a little while, you enter the shop to be greeted with: "I'm afraid you'll have to come back later. I am very busy," then you have to do some quick thinking, because either the buyer is using this sentence as a stock sentence to get rid of you, or he really is busy and, therefore, it's a waste of time trying to sell to him.

In a recent analysis taken from two hundred shopkeepers, a hundred and thirty of them admitted that more often than not they were not as busy as they appeared to be, and they were using the 'busy' excuse just to get rid of the salesman. This, of course, is nonsense, because the shopkeeper is there to make money, and the salesman has called to help him make money.

If, for example, the salesman were to walk into the shop and hold out a pound note and tell the shopkeeper he could have it for fifty pence, the shopkeeper might think him crazy, but he wouldn't say that he was too busy to deal with the matter.

It is only a question, therefore, if the buyer is misleading you, of working out an approach sentence which will arouse his interest before he has a chance to tell you that he is too busy.

I'LL BE WITH YOU SOON

At our training courses we train men for many of the leading companies selling staple goods. Often, these salesmen have been in the habit of writing letters to their customers before a journey, telling them the time and date on which they will be calling. Subsequently, when we have advised them to drop this system, they have found an improvement in their turnover.

The reason for this is that quite often they receive a reply advising them that as nothing is required there is no need for a call to be made. This is not necessarily true, however, as many a salesman has proved. All it may mean is that the customer is buying from someone else, and does not want to be bothered to see the salesman.

Alternatively, a buyer might send his order through the post, and it may be a very small order in comparison to the kind the salesman would have taken if he had made the call.

Experiment—cut out these appointment letters, and just call.

YOU WILL MEET THEM OVER COFFEE

"Good morning," he says, looking a bit gloomy. "Rotten morning, isn't it?"

"Yes," you answer, "it isn't too good."

"Been on this territory long?" he asks.

"Not very long," you answer.

You both sip your coffee in silence for a few moments, and then he says, "Things are bad, aren't they?"

"Well——" you begin.

But he interrupts with, "I honestly don't know what the end's going to be. Trade's getting worse and worse. Shops are all stocked up."

You can meet this type of man in any coffee shop. He is a complete misery, and if you sit with him for long you will become as miserable as he is—and you will sell badly because of that. If you don't sit next to him at coffee, maybe you'll be sitting next to another type. . . .

"How are things?" he asks.

"Not too bad," you answer, although you may not really be doing too well.

"I think they're better than ever," he says. "I've just been calling on Bill. (Bill is the Christian name of the managing director of the leading company in the town.) I took an order for five thousand . . . I'm just on my way to see Charlie. (Charlie is one of the leading store buyers in town.) I always say to him, 'Charlie,' I say, 'I can let you have six gross.' He takes it like a lamb."

This type of salesman will often produce a bunch of papers from his inner pocket to denote the number of orders he has taken that day. He will never, however, show you the orders. It's all done by implication.

Now this man is nothing more or less than a first-rate liar who likes to hear himself talk, and likes to feel important. He can be more depressing than the despondent salesman, because he can make you dissatisfied with your job, as he conveys the impression that he is earning about five times as much as you are. Once a salesman gets it into his mind that he ought to look for a better job, he becomes unsettled, sells badly, and may lose his job and not get a better one.

Yes, perhaps it is nice to meet the boys over coffee, but it is far wiser not to be one of the boys. Just be a man, and don't let these people waste your time.

SUBTERFUGE

Should a salesman use subterfuge to enable him to get an interview? The answer is NO. The only subterfuge he may use legitimately is when giving his own name in preference to the name of his company.

J. A. Barrett of the Norwich Union Life Insurance Society put the case quite clearly. "Only once," he said, "did I use subterfuge. I inferred to the secretary that I had called because a mutual friend had suggested that I call, and on those grounds I was seen by the managing director. At the interview, because my conscience was not clear, I started off badly, made a bad sale, and, in fact, got away as quickly as I could."

In other words, only the salesman who isn't worried about misrepresentation can get away with subterfuge. As his days are numbered anyway, taken all round it can be said that honesty in getting the interview always pays.

SEE THE MAN WHO CAN BUY

SCENE: *The office of a managing director. There is a knock at the door, and the office manager walks in.*

MANAGING DIRECTOR: "Good morning, Whelks."

OFFICE MANAGER: "Good morning, Mr. Barr. I've got something this morning that I really think is going to increase our efficiency and bring us increased profits."

BARR: "Good! We're always on the look-out for that sort of thing. I hope it isn't going to cost us anything, though. Shortage of money, you know. Must watch capital expenditure. What is it?"

WHELKS (*producing a leaflet*): "Here it is. It's a new kind of printing machine—turns out first-class work—and you know we're spending a great deal on printing. I think it will cut down our costs considerably."

BARR (*nods his head*): "Yes, go on. Tell me some more."

Whelks tells him some more—in fact he tells him quite a lot more. Then the managing director asks, "And what is the price?"

"Only six thousand," answers the office manager.

"What!" the managing director barks. "Six thousand pounds? Do you think we're made of money? Where do you think the money is coming from? All I hear is that somebody wants a car, a typist needs a new typewriter, a clerk must have another desk. . . . It's quite ridiculous the way money is being spent in this organisation. Oh, I'm not saying it isn't a good machine, but I'm not spending six thousand pounds."

And so Whelks departs.

Now let us look at a similar scene. Managing director Barr is sitting at his desk. He moves a switch on his intercommunicating telephone, and rings through to his office manager. "Whelks," he said, "come down and see me for a minute, will you?"

A minute afterwards Whelks arrives.

"Good morning, sir," he says brightly.

"Ah, good morning, Whelks. I want to tell you about something that I've just hit upon—an extremely good idea—the very thing you need for your department."

"Oh, yes, sir," says Whelks. "What is it?"

"Well," answers Barr, "it's a new kind of printing machine. I saw it at the exhibition—it's a first-class job. Look, this is it."

He hands Whelks the leaflet.

"Yes," says Whelks, "I've heard about these."

"Oh, they're excellent! You know our printing bills are colossal, we really must try to cut them down. I had the salesman call to see me about half an hour ago and, quite frankly, he convinced me that it's an excellent proposition. I think we ought to go ahead, don't you?"

"Well, yes, of course, sir. But—er—how much is it?"

"Oh, only six thousand pounds."

"Six thousand pounds!" says Whelks. "That seems a lot of money."

"A lot of money?" says the managing director. "Six thousand pounds a lot of money? Why, what's six thousand pounds in an organisation such as ours? You must remember, Whelks, that in business you have to spend money to earn money. After all, where would I have been to-day if I had listened to my accountants and my bank manager, and never troubled to invest a penny in this, or a pound in that? No, Whelks, that's a lesson that you've got to learn. Sometimes you have to spend money to increase your profits, you know. I think we ought to buy it."

"Yes, sir," says Whelks, being a sensible office manager. "I think, probably, it will be most valuable to us."

And so the salesman gets an order for a printing machine.

Now what lessons are you going to learn from those two scenes? Obvious, aren't they? *You must always sell to the man who can buy.* Don't be put off by assistants, senior clerks, or anyone who is not in authority. On many occasions you do have to sell to a manager, but in nearly every organisation of average size, and in quite a few of the larger organisations as well, the managing director is the only man who can sanction any large form of capital outlay. If the proposition is put to him, he is much more likely to buy than if he hears about it from another person.

If you do have to sell to an office manager, then you must fight for an appointment with the managing director himself, so that you are able to sell to him. The rule for every salesman is:

YOU MUST TELL YOUR STORY TO THE MAN ON TOP.

THAT FIGHTING SPIRIT

When I asked F. H. Jenkins, sales director of the Kleen-e-ze Brush Company Ltd., to what he attributed his success, he answered, "I always fought back."

Some salesmen don't like the idea of using the word 'fight' in connection with salesmanship. They think it savours too much of high-pressure methods. As I have consistently taught low-pressure selling for so many years, no one can accuse me of believing in high-pressure selling. I do, however, believe in fighting salesmanship.

It is the normal reaction of most people not to want to buy anything. Shopkeepers invariably seem to be stocked up. Those who purchase capital equipment never seem to have any money to spend. When these excuses are advanced, however, they are really brought forward as a challenge. The prospect or shopkeeper is really saying, "I don't think I want your goods, but if you put up a fight I might listen to you." If he is uncertain about buying he is going to fight hard against placing the order—*and the salesman must fight back.*

Most of all, however, the fighting spirit in salesmanship is not connected with the actual obtaining of the order. I think what Jenkins meant was the ability to keep on keeping on when things are tough.

When young men want to become salesmen they visualise a life in the open, the sun streaming down while they drive their luxury cars about the country. They think of nice comfortable hotels, and of cheery conversations with their fellow salesmen around a blazing fire in the evenings. Maybe they think of romance now and again. They do not, however, think of the days when the snow lies thick on the ground; when they have a slight chill; when nobody wants to buy anything, and they have to slog it out on foot because they are not selling well enough to afford a car.

It is because they don't think on these lines that they are so quickly knocked off their feet when they meet the first rough passage.

Because of his enthusiasm in doing something new, many a young salesman starts off by selling well. When orders become fewer, his enthusiasm wanes; and when he meets conditions such as I have described it disappears completely.

It is only those young men possessed of the fighting spirit who do, then, fight back to regain their enthusiasm and can go on to achieve success.

MEET THE SECRETARY

"Could I see Mr. Brown for a few minutes?"

"Please tell Mr. Brown that I have something that I am sure will interest him."

"I represent the ABC Company. I am quite sure your people want to hear what I have to tell them."

"You can be sure I wouldn't waste his time, if only he would spare me just a minute or two. . . ."

And similar sentences by the dozen are used every day. Some salesmen seem to think that a secretary is just another system of inter-office communication, employed only to take messages to her boss.

That is all wrong. One of her functions is to keep time-wasters away from her chief, and this she usually does most efficiently. You must make her feel important. When you adopt this attitude you are not flattering. The secretary is a very vital part of any organisation, and if she sees you in the waiting-room and asks you your business you should say, "I'm so glad you've come out yourself to see me. I should like to explain to you briefly what I want to see Mr. X. about, and I know you'll agree that my proposition will interest him." Then, very briefly, explain your proposition. Use a potted sales sequence, but sell strongly. When you have finished, add, "That, briefly, is what I wanted to say to Mr. X. You will agree that it will save the firm quite a lot of money. But, anyway, I wanted to ask your advice—don't you think he would like to hear my proposition?"

When you ask for advice in this manner, in more cases than not she will arrange an appointment for you to see her chief.

The best way to handle a secretary is to ask for her advice.

CONTACTS

Most salesmen like the idea of contacts. They are always pleased when a customer suggests that they call on a friend who might place an order with them. A salesman may have twelve or fifteen such contacts given to him during the course of a year. He could double or treble this amount. In fact, his contacts could run into hundreds if he went the right way about it.

A past master at this is Jack Holmes, who works for an associate company of ours. He believes in talking about his business to every one he meets. He talks to strangers in trains (one such chat resulted in his obtaining the biggest order of his career), to managers in restaurants, to anyone who can spare him a few minutes.

Knowing the way people react to strangers talking to them in trains you may think this is rather a foolish idea, but this is the way Jack puts it: "People don't like talking to strangers because they are afraid of being bored. The reason why people don't talk about their own job is because an Englishman is naturally rather reserved and conventional, and it goes against the grain to talk about himself or the work he does. Well," says Jack, "I'm not ashamed of my job, and I find that when I do talk to other people about it they are deeply interested, and that is the way I have obtained dozens and dozens of new contacts. *I talk about my products to everyone I meet.*"

That is sound advice for all salesmen. You will not bore anyone when you talk about your work if you are interesting enough. Every conversation could lead to a new contact.

THE PROBLEM

The room wasn't very well furnished, the curtains certainly needed a clean, but then the boarding house wasn't very expensive. I always stayed there on my visits to Glasgow.

In the room were two other salesmen besides myself. We were all climbing the ladder to success, but there were still very many rungs to be climbed.

Harrison, who sold baby wear, was playing patience, and cheating quite a lot from what I could see.

I was thinking about the calls I had to make next day.

Arthur Price was sitting back in the solitary armchair, gazing at the ceiling.

"A penny for them, Arthur," I said. "What's she like?"

"I was thinking about business," was his answer.

"Haven't you worked out your calls yet?"

"Of course I have! I was thinking about just one call."

"Well, I'm thinking of them all," I said.

"You just keep on thinking, and leave me to my thoughts."

"What's so important about this one call?" I queried.

"Every call's important," he said, "but before I visit anyone I don't think so much about my side of the picture—I think of the other side. I'm going to Wellwyn's in the morning. They aren't easy people, and I'm trying to work out their problems.

When I've got them all lined up, I think I shall know how to get an order."

I learned a lesson that day that I've never forgotten. When a salesman is planning his work he should always give preference of thought to his customers' problems. When he knows what they are up against he can make a sale.

To the good salesman the customers' problems are his problems.

THOSE NEW-FANGLED THINGS

Years ago, when telephones were first used, owners of business premises said, "Those new-fangled things? Not for me!"

It would be a good idea if some of our present-day salesmen were to think on these lines, if only for one reason—to make them realise that although a telephone is an essential in business to-day, it can do a great deal of harm if a salesman misuses it.

The one time a telephone is more misused than any other is when it is used at the request of a prospective buyer. If all salesmen who didn't get their orders because prospects told them to 'ring me up' were put side by side, they would stretch from here to—well, it doesn't matter where, but it would be a long way away!

The prospect sounds so friendly when he pats you on the shoulder and says, "Yes, I'll get this tied up for you. Just give me a ring to-morrow, and I'll tell you how many I need." Or, "Ring me in three days' time. I'll give you my final decision then. It's almost bound to be yes, but . . ." and so on.

What has happened is that the prospect is using the telephone as a get-out because he knows that it is so much easier to say "No" over the telephone than it is when confronted by a salesman who puts his case in a logical manner. When, therefore, the telephone-happy salesman dials a number and receives a turndown it's an awful shock to him. It probably puts him off selling for the whole of the day.

In future, when you are asked to telephone, DON'T. Make some excuse. Say that you will be passing that day and will just look in; or, better still, look in anyway. But at all costs try to avoid telephoning when a final decision is at stake.

SELL THE TYPIST

There's a well-known business selling carbons and ribbons which was built up by the perseverance and efforts of one man who made headway even during the 1950 recession. He started selling office supplies after leaving the army, where he had been a regular officer for a number of years. He found the going extremely tough. Office managers were not interested in him, and neither were managing directors.

Then he hit on the idea of selling to the typist. Whenever he made a call he made a big effort to see one of the typists, or, if the manager had a secretary, he tried to see the secretary. He would go to endless trouble to please the typists, to let them try out various carbons; to enable him to get their opinions. Later, automatically, they recommended his goods.

It is always essential to tell your sales story to the man who can buy, but it is sometimes a very good plan to sell your ideas to the people in an organisation who are going to use the equipment. For example, if you are selling a service for the use of the maintenance engineer, then sell that maintenance engineer on the idea of your service before you sell the managing director. Don't let the maintenance engineer sell the proposition for you, but get him on your side, so that when you do eventually see the managing director and he refers to the maintenance engineer, the engineer will agree that your equipment will be of value to him.

DON'T LET MEMBERS OF THE STAFF DO YOUR SELLING FOR YOU, BUT SELL THEM ON THE IDEA OF YOUR PRODUCTS.

DEAD HORSES

Too many salesmen waste too much time calling on customers or prospects who are useless to them. I firmly believe in stickability, and that a salesman should make every attempt to sell to every prospect he calls on. He should continue to call, if necessary, week after week, month after month, to try to get an order. He is justified in calling, provided that every time he calls he can make an honest attempt to obtain the order. Generally speaking, however, when a salesman has called too often on a customer or prospect, he no longer attempts to sell. They have a friendly discussion, talk about this and that, the salesman mentions his products as if he doesn't really expect to get an order, and then departs.

That's what I call flogging a dead horse. When the time comes that you can no longer sell in a proper orderly sequence to a prospect and hold his attention while you are selling— then give up selling.

WHAT'S THE USE OF GOODWILL?

Some men can be perfectly trained in salesmanship, and still fail hopelessly, because they never say, "Does that apply to me?" They always know better than their teachers. They feel that there is some short cut to success, and they are going to take it.

I remember we had such a salesman some little while ago, and this story only proves that even with the most careful methods of selection and training, mistakes can be made.

The salesman was told at the school that the only way he would get orders was to tell a complete sales story at every call. A few days after he started working for us a friend of mine who owns a restaurant telephoned me and asked me whether I employed postmen instead of salesmen. I didn't understand what he meant until he said that that morning one of our leaflets (one which cost us about thirty pence, at that) had been pushed through his letter-box.

I couldn't understand what had happened, so I sent a manager over to investigate. He found that every business house in the street had also had a leaflet put through the letter-box.

Yes, the culprit was the new salesman. I sent for him and asked him why he had done it, and he answered, "Well, it all creates goodwill, Mr. Tack. I can't be everywhere at once. These people will see the leaflet, and sooner or later they will get in touch with us."

I reminded him of the fact that the average circularising campaign only brought in about one and a half per cent enquiries, and therefore he would have to put thousands and thousands of leaflets through letter-boxes to get an inquiry, and that we didn't pay him his salary to do that. I said that he was paid to sell, and there was no short cut to making the calls. . . .

Too many salesmen think that they create goodwill which will lead to further sales by leaving leaflets with prospects or customers. These leaflets are rarely read. Generally, they find their way quickly into the waste-paper basket. So don't be a leaflet-dropper.

The only time you should leave a leaflet is either when you have made a sale, to cement confidence, or when you have told your whole story, fought very hard for the order, but failed to pull it off. In the latter case a leaflet might help the prospect to make up his mind before your next call.

HABITS

It has been said that anyone can be successful if prepared to pay a price for success, but very few are prepared to pay any price whatsoever.

I have known salesmen who have done extraordinarily well, although their actions have been against all known teachings on salesmanship. Some may not have cared for their appearance. Others have been heavy drinkers, and so on. But remember, these are rare exceptions, and the average man will do well not to attempt to copy them or to think that that is the way to be successful. Men of that type are very few and far between.

Most of us have to pay some price to achieve success. For instance, we often have to reorganise our habits. You can be a more successful salesman if you develop the RIGHT habits.

Here are just a few that are well worth bearing in mind:

1. Get up early.
2. Don't turn a cold into the 'flu.

By that I mean, very few people stay at home these days with a cold—they always have the 'flu. I have seen so many report sheets from salesmen containing this item of news: *In bed with 'flu*. I know it's the right medical advice always to stay in bed if you have a little sniffle, but very few of us can do this. The majority of us have to go on working, and it's the same with a salesman. If you don't feel up to scratch when you wake up in the morning—if you have a little headache or just a slight cold, don't mislead yourself into thinking that you have influenza. Don't form the bad habit of giving up too easily.

3. Never spend more than five minutes on your morning coffee or afternoon tea. Never spend more than half an hour a day on lunch during a working week.

MAKE MORE CALLS

Do this:

1. When you decide to finish a day's work—make one more call.
2. Whatever time you start work now, start earlier so that you can make one more call.
3. Cut down your lunch time so that you can make one more call.
4. You would complain bitterly if your company cut your commission. Time wasters you meet when on the road STEAL YOUR MONEY. Don't let them waste your time— MAKE ONE MORE CALL INSTEAD.
5. However many calls a day you are now making re-plan your day to make one more call.

MORE CALLS MEAN MORE SALES

CHAPTER V

Sales Techniques Used by Top Salesmen

ALL salesmen know that one demonstration is worth a thousand words. They also appreciate the value of well-thought-out literature and good samples. What is often overlooked, however, is the fact that these sales aids and samples by themselves can never effect a sale. They are an adjunct to the salesman's words. A salesman lives by his words. If one set of words will help him more than another, then obviously he will use those which serve him best.

This chapter is designed to help the salesman to improve his sales technique.

THREE WAYS OF BUILDING A SALES SEQUENCE

Once having mastered a sales sequence, a salesman achieves greater confidence, begins to enjoy his salesmanship, and his sales increase. Irrespective of the product being sold, the sales executive should provide his salesmen with a sales story. Yes, this applies to salesmen calling regularly on their customers just as much as to speciality salesmen.

A sales sequence cannot, however, be developed by sitting at an office desk. Theories are no good. A story can only be evolved from hard practical experience, and every sales manager who has been off the road for any length of time should return to selling, for a week anyway, before building up a new sales sequence. Then about every three months he should revise that sales sequence in the light of new developments, and he should always call in his managers or leading salesmen for consultation regarding the suggested revision.

Here are three ways to develop a sales sequence:

1. *The Monologue*

Find out all the reasons why the prospect or the buyer should place an order for the goods you are selling. Discover all the benefits to him of handling your goods. Write these down separately, and then elaborate them in your own language until you have built up a complete monologue of the sale. Learn this by heart until you can repeat it verbatim.

Spend a week selling only by using this monologue, and never deviating from it by one word except, of course, to help to sell yourself or talk about the prospect's interests. During the week try to find out if there are any points which you have left out; then, after a week's try-out, re-write the whole story to make certain that you have it as complete as possible.

An individual salesman can make good use of the self-developed monologue. If, however, a salesman is taught selling in this way, he is trying to learn the language of someone else—the sales manager or another executive. This often results in a salesman sounding very much like a parrot. He's uninspiring, he lacks enthusiasm, and he doesn't put over his story with conviction.

That is one of the disadvantages with the monologue sales sequence. It is only good when a salesman develops it himself.

2. *The Duologue*

In developing this type of sales sequence, the salesman builds his narrative up by asking his imaginary prospect a question at the end of each selling point. He then gives an answer to each question as he thinks a prospect will be likely to reply. In this way he learns both parts of the sales story—his part and the prospect's.

This type of sequence was taught for some time, but it was not really successful because none of us can be mind readers. We are never certain that we are going to get the right answers to the questions that we put to the prospect.

The advantage of this type of sales sequence is that it does make the salesman follow a golden rule of selling, which is to ask questions. The disadvantage is that the salesman is likely to be put out of his stride if the prospect doesn't react as he should.

3. *The Selling Sentence*

The selling-sentence sequence is probably the best of all for teaching a sales story. It is also the easiest way in which a salesman can develop the best possible story, and ally it to his own personality.

To develop this sales sequence the salesman must first of all divide his story up into several steps. The main ones should be:

1. The Approach
2. Creation of Interest
3. Creation of Confidence
4. Selling the Product
5. The Close

The step SELLING THE PRODUCT would probably have to be subdivided into perhaps four or five different steps to cover each of the main points about the article being sold.

A good selling sentence is then developed to give the lead in to each step.

Memory training experts tell us that one of the easiest ways to learn is by the association of ideas. Once a salesman has given his selling sentence to lead him into his step, then he will be able to elaborate on that theme at some length, and the words will be his own—they won't be the words of his sales manager or a teacher of salesmanship.

In developing this idea, the salesman should think of any sales aids which he might use, and he should ally these to his sentences. It isn't very difficult to memorise perhaps a dozen sentences—not nearly so difficult as trying to remember a complete sales story—but so long as the salesman does remember them, and keeps to the sequence, elaborating each step with interest and enthusiasm, then he will develop the best possible sales story.

Remember, there is no substitute for a good sales sequence, and the selling-sentence technique is the most satisfactory method of enabling a salesman to develop his best possible story. Great care, however, must be given to working out really strong selling sentences.

BE POSITIVE

The managing director of a firm of advertising agents called to see me to ask me to vet his sales sequence for him. Now advertising people are taught that they must always be positive in their appeal, but the sales story I was shown was full of 'possibly's' and 'maybe's'. One sentence was: *I may be able to help you*; another, *I can't tell what results I can bring about until I have spent a few days with you*; and other similar negative sentences.

That is bad selling. If a salesman is as confident in his products as he ought to be, then he should be able to state categorically that if the prospect places an order with him, that prospect will benefit.

Far better for the advertising expert to have said, *When we have designed this brochure for you it will help your salesmen to sell more.*

Go through your sales talk with a tooth comb. Cut out every word—every sentence—which has a half-hearted appeal. Salesmen must be positive at all times.

DON'T BE A WONDERER

Too many salesmen use words or expressions which should never be used in selling. For example: "I wonder if this would do?" or, "I wonder if the display would look better if it were put in the window this way?" or, "I wonder, if you took a 6-in. double instead of a 3-in. double, whether the results would be more than twice as good?"

No buyer wants to deal with wonderers. They want to be told by the salesman what his product can do for them. If the salesman has ideas they want to hear those ideas in a concrete form.

"I wonder . . ." will only leave the prospect wondering.

NINE SENTENCES WHICH SELL

A salesman lives by his words! It always amazes me to hear how little thought most men give to the words they use. They gabble on and on, without a thought of the punch sentences which would make all the difference to the sale.

Here are some words to remember—they always click with a prospect:

"*It's new*"—we all like to hear of something new. When you say to a prospect, "This unit heater is new and . . ." you hold his interest.

"*Up to the minute*"—another very good expression. When you refer to your research department, to your factory, or to your service as being 'up to the minute', you are using words with a punch!

"*Special*"—here is another very good selling word. "This is something special, sir"—maybe you are referring to your sample, perhaps to your leaflet—but it rivets attention.

"*Discovery*"—another excellent word. We are all interested in something newly discovered.

"*Saves*"—here is another good word. "It saves you time"; "It saves you worry"; "It saves you money"; "It saves your customers". . . . Yes, remember that word!

"*You*"—the most powerful selling word of all! "*Your home*"; "*Your shop*"; "*Your family*"; "*Your customers*"—you cannot sell well without using such expressions.

"*Immediate*"—another good word. "The results are immediate." It's better than *quick* or *fast*. They are too indefinite.

"*Thank you*"—don't forget that we all like to be thanked for what we do. Even during a sale your prospect will say or do something which will give you the opportunity to say "Thank you", and he likes to hear it.

WHY?

One of my companies issues a daily bulletin, and a little while ago they announced a competition for their salesmen. The competition invited salesmen to write an essay on: *What is the most important word in selling?*

Here is the prize-winning entry:

". . . I didn't really think that any one word in selling was more important than another, until I read the bulletin. Honestly, I hadn't given the matter a thought, that's why it had never come to my mind that one particular word might be of great importance. I wanted to win the prize, so without any hesitation I wrote down the word: YOU—and I was just about to send it off when I had second thoughts.

"YOU, in selling, is certainly a very important word. It means that the salesman is talking in terms of the other man's interests. But I wasn't certain whether it was *the* most important word. On second thoughts, I decided on BUT. What would a salesman do when answering objections if it were not for that magic word BUT? How many times had I swung a sale in my favour, just by using it and then answering the objection. Yes, obviously BUT was going to be my winning word.

"But wait a moment—that might not win the competition. After all, a NAME is a word. The prospect's name, surely, is as important as anything. Yes, that would probably win. . . . But perhaps it wouldn't, because I have obtained many a sale where I did not use the prospect's name quite as much as I should have done.

"I went on thinking of word after word, until I decided not to enter for the competition until I'd made another call.

"While I was making my next sale I listened to myself selling. That sounds rather silly, but I did listen to myself saying various words.

"I watched the buyer's reactions to the words I was using, and when I had finished that sale I knew what my entry was going to be. Yes, there is one word better than all the others. It's a wonderful word—it's the word

WHY

That's the word which helps the sale along. That's the word which can switch a losing sales talk into a winning one. That's the word which makes a depressing buyer into a cheerful fellow. That's the word to turn the silent prospect into a talker. Yes, that's the word which wins sales.

"WHY?—WELL, I'VE JUST TOLD YOU. . . ."

AND THE MESSAGE IS . . .

Most of us have played the game of whispering in one of its many forms. The one I like commences with somebody in the party thinking up a sentence and whispering it to the person seated next to him. He in turn whispers it to his neighbour, and the message is passed on in this way, right round the room, until the last person receives it and repeats it aloud. The message received at the end of the line generally bears no resemblance at all to the original message.

I was reminded of this game when a salesman called to see me to sell me a certain type of office equipment. I didn't expect him to be a technical engineer, but I did expect him to know something about his product, and when he failed to answer two or three quite ordinary questions I felt rather sorry for him.

Obviously, no one had gone to the trouble of giving him all the facts about his equipment, and he was, perhaps, a little too raw to realise that he should have obtained these facts before he could start to sell. The manufacturers of the machine know every detail of their product. They pass on this information to a distributor—in this case the firm in question were the sole distributors.

Obviously, the manufacturers' story had lost something in the telling to the distributor. They, in turn, employed various agents throughout the country. Once again, quite a lot must have been left out of the story by the time the distributor had explained the main points to his agents.

The agents employed salesmen but, by the time the agents had been armed with all the knowledge they could obtain about the product, they were a long way short of the manufacturers' knowledge. All the way down the line something was being lost, until the salesman's knowledge of the machine was almost negligible.

A salesman must thoroughly understand his product. He should attempt to know as much about it as does the manufacturer himself. Although he will always sell WHAT THE PRODUCT WILL DO rather than how it is actually made; the fact that he knows how it is made will allow him, by an odd word here and there, to set himself up as an expert at his job.

He would never be so foolish as to use this knowledge to bore prospects with long details about his equipment. Nobody wants to hear that. Nor would he tell potential buyers how little they know. But he would use it to strengthen his sales story, and to be able to answer any questions which might be put to him by a buyer who knows as much as he does about his product.

DON'T DEPEND ON HIS MEMORY

"Most people," says sales manager Charles Short, "have bad memories. It is for that reason that salesmen must continually emphasise and re-emphasise their strong selling points. When a salesman has been with a prospect for some time he has spoken so many words that the prospect's mind is probably muddled, and not at all clear about the whole proposition. So," says Charles, "every few minutes, go back over your sales talk and repeat with conviction your strongest selling point. Then, when you get towards the end of the sale, repeat them all over again. Far better to risk slightly boring a customer by emphasising these points than to go on just talking and talking and completely bewilder him."

DON'T ISSUE A CHALLENGE

"At some time or another you'll have to buy, so you might just as well have it now."

That might be a perfectly true statement. The customer may know it to be true, but the fact that the salesman has made it may make the customer willing to lose money rather than place an order for that particular line of goods.

Few men like to admit defeat, and this statement implies that at some time or another the salesman is going to defeat the prospect instead of trying to win him over by logical argument. So don't use this type of sentence when selling.

I WANT IT

What do you want right now? A new television set? A motor mower? A new suit?

But what do you need right now? Maybe your car needs respraying badly, but perhaps you're not very interested in your car. You just use it for your work, and you don't mind very much what it looks like. Still, it does need that respray. But it's going to cost you three hundred to respray your car, and you could get a colour television for that.

Well, which are you going to have?

If you were faced with that problem it's almost certain that you would choose the television set, and make yourself believe that the car would go on for another year or so without having to be resprayed.

We're all like that. We buy, in the main, the things we want, and we put off buying the things we need, if we can't have both.

The salesman, therefore, must be a creator of wants. He has often been called a *want-maker* because he has to make the prospect want to place an order with him. The prospect may need new linoleum for his shop, and you may be trying to sell him fluorescent lighting. You have to make him want your fluorescent lighting more than he feels he needs the linoleum. A retailer may only have a certain amount of money to spend on books. The salesman of books might have to make that bookseller realise that although he may need books on bird life, he should place an order for a best seller, because that would result in a quicker turnover for him. So the salesman has to make the bookseller *want* to stock the best seller rather than the books on bird life.

No matter what you are selling, similar instances will occur. The first-class salesman must always be a *maker of wants*.

YOUR SENTENCES MUST CREATE CONFIDENCE

Have you ever said of a doctor, "It's no use calling him in, I haven't any confidence in him"?

Now the doctor in whom you have no confidence has received exactly the same amount of training as any other doctor, and the possibility is that he is an extremely good G.P. He has, however, failed in one respect. He has not won your confidence, and therefore, whatever medicine he gives you, whatever advice he offers, will not have the same effect upon you as it would have if you had faith in him.

A brilliant doctor with a practice in the East End of London told me that his patients often recovered more rapidly because he refused to 'sit on a fence'.

In fully ninety per cent of the calls made by a general practitioner the complaints are of a minor character which can be quickly diagnosed and dealt with quite simply. If my doctor friend was puzzled then, obviously, he would call for another opinion. But with the average call he always instilled confidence in the patient by telling him that the medicine he had prescribed would soon put him right, or that he had nothing to worry about. To put it more simply, he doesn't scare patients into thinking that they are really ill when they are not. After all, that isn't so very different from the mother dealing with the child who has fallen down, hurt his hand, and is crying. She picks up the child, kisses the hand and says, "There, that's all better now!" and the child stops crying. His confidence has been restored.

In the same way as a patient reacts favourably to a doctor who wins his confidence, or a child is quickly restored to smiles when its confidence is restored, so the prospect buys more easily and more readily when he has confidence in the salesman.

Some salesmen do go to some trouble to create confidence at their first call. They talk about the reputation of their company, or their advertising programme; they discuss their company's research plant, and so on. But then, when they call back subsequently, they forget to go on creating confidence.

Salesmen must remember that they must create and maintain confidence at every call. There are many, many commercial travellers tramping the streets to-day who never will become successful, because a lot of their so-called friends in the trade have no real confidence either in their ability, in their sales reputation, or their companies. These men have never gone to the trouble of creating any confidence. In fact, the reverse—if ever they could moan about something, they have moaned, and that is a sure way of breaking down confidence.

Make it a rule from now on to create confidence at every call, and stick to that rule.

FOUR SENTENCES TO HELP YOU TO CREATE CONFIDENCE

The speciality salesman must create confidence immediately after he has made his approach. He must again win more confidence in himself when the order is near the close. But whatever we are selling, whatever we are doing, there are certain sentences which will always help a salesman to create confidence. Here are a few of them:

1. Your friend, Mr. Smith, asked me to call to see you, as he felt sure that I could be helpful to you.
2. We are doubling our advertising expenditure on this line in the next two months.
3. The craftsmen who manufacture this apparatus are backed by over eighty years' experience—men whose fathers before them carried out the same work.
4. I have never before handled a line which has sold so rapidly.

These are typical sentences which are used regularly by salesmen. They are given to you as a guide. Work out your own confidence-creating sentences and use them.

HAS YOUR CUSTOMER A GOOD MEMORY?

"One of the biggest shocks I ever had when selling," recounts Alfred Hayes, now sales director of a perfumery company, "happened when I was selling lawn mowers many years ago.

"My biggest account was a firm of hardware merchants in

the Midlands, and I was on very friendly terms with the managing director, who did all his own buying, although he didn't do the selling.

"One day, I made my usual routine call, fully prepared to book a big order for the spring, and I was greeted by the managing director, who looked, I thought, a little sheepish. I soon learned why when he said to me, 'I'm afraid we're giving you a miss for next season. I've decided to run . . .' and he mentioned a competitor's make.

"'Whatever made you do that?' I asked. 'I've given you good service. We advertise extensively. We've been good friends for years. . . .'

"We talked for some time, and in the end the truth emerged. My competitor, by pointing out a special feature of their new model, had won him over. It was a feature for rapidly adjusting the cutting blades.

"At that I quite exploded. 'But,' I said, 'we've had that for the last three years!'

"'Have you?' he answered. 'I didn't know.'

"'Well,' I said, 'I'm sure your assistants know. After all, they demonstrate them regularly.'

"'Yes,' he mumbled, 'they probably do, they probably do, but—er—I didn't really take it up with them. I was very impressed with . . .' and he went on to say how impressed he was with the other make. But I knew, in my heart, that the real reason he had shifted was because the other salesman had stressed the importance of that adjustment, and how it would help him to sell more mowers, and that if he didn't stock them his customers would go elsewhere, and so on. Anyway, I lost the contract."

"Did you ever get it back?" I asked Hayes.

"Only partly," he answered. "We were never on the same footing again. After all, I'd made him look a little foolish by telling him that our mowers had a feature about which he wasn't aware, but, of course, the fault was really mine."

"For telling him that he was wrong?" I asked.

"Not only that. For relying on his memory. We should never rely on a customer's or prospect's memory. Every time we call we should stress the advantages of our products, and its special features—just as a reminder. If we don't do that he forgets about them—and then one day we lose the order."

You can thank Alfred Hayes for this first-rate lesson in salesmanship.

Never rely on the customer's memory. Keep him up to date with all new developments of your products, but always remind him over and over again of the special features which have proved his wisdom in buying from you.

WHAT DO YOU LEAVE OUT?

Garthwaite is the sales manager of a firm selling soaps and soap powders to grocers. His company train their salesmen adequately. Whenever a man was slipping, Garthwaite was in the habit of sending him with one of his best salesmen to watch how a sale should be conducted. He got quite good results.

Then one day he had a brainwave. He said to me subsequently, "You know a salesman doesn't learn a great deal when listening to someone else. Just to stand aside as a stooge doesn't help him a lot."

Garthwaite told me that what he did was to send a salesman whose turnover was dropping with a man who was not a first-class salesman.

"This is what happened," he said. "I told Salesman A. to work with Salesman X., which surprised him, because X. was not very experienced. He went with him, and then I asked him to come to see me at the office. 'Well,' I said to A., 'how did you enjoy yourself?' 'It was all right,' he said, 'but, you know, I just couldn't keep quiet. It was awful to hear him missing this out, and forgetting that. I kept having to jump in myself, to help him out. He wasn't telling half his story.'

"Then," said Garthwaite to Salesman A., "you have learned a good lesson. You have seen a man in action, and you've seen why he's not getting more orders. He's forgetting half his sales story. You, when you were with him, were anxious to help him out. You could see his mistakes. Now just imagine if someone else were with you and they heard you selling. They would also want to jump in because you would be missing out parts of your sales story. The reason why your figures have dropped is because you have been cutting down your sales story."

Garthwaite told me that he had achieved excellent results by letting salesmen watch other men of less sales ability than themselves in action. That made them think.

If your figures aren't as good as they should be, approach your sales manager and ask him to let you work with one of the other salesmen—not one of the top notchers. You will be able to see what they are leaving out of their sales story, and that will remind you of what you are leaving out of yours.

BE PREPARED

It might be a good thing if every salesman became a scout. Why? Because the motto of the scouts is BE PREPARED. Too many salesmen don't trouble to prepare anything. Look at their selling kits. Examine their samples, and you will find that they are not always as they should be.

I have known many a man, punctilious about his appearance, living in a well-conducted house, yet with a sales kit which was a perfect disgrace. An old battered bag—there's nothing wrong with that—but it is very bad when the bag is stained, the buckles coming off, and the literature inside it dog-eared and dirty.

If you had to make a speech this evening you would give careful thought to it. It would, perhaps, worry you all day long. You would think of little else but that speech. You would obviously make notes or even write out the speech in full. I have never met a man yet who was asked to make a speech and who didn't go to some trouble to prepare it. It's just as necessary for every salesman to prepare for his sale.

He should develop the habit of checking over his complete sales kit every week-end—not just once a month, but every week-end. That should be a careful, searching check. Then every *night* he should glance through his bag to see if anything needs to be replaced.

He will obviously prepare to work his territory, but that is dealt with separately. The other point about being prepared is to think up new sales angles, and new selling sentences continually.

Always keep to your sales sequence—that is essential. But before you make any special call, just turn over in your mind what questions you are likely to be asked, and see whether you can think of any good sales points for that prospect's trade.

Be Prepared is a good motto for the salesman.

PLUG IT!

A salesman who works to a sales sequence should give the whole sequence every time. One or two details may not have to be discussed at length, but he *must* remember to use EVERY SALES POINT.

The good salesman, however, always watches for the *main* item of interest. By this I mean that during the sale he may notice that one of his sales points obviously arouses the prospect's interest. He should plug that for all he's worth, and keep on plugging it right through the sale. When you do this, however, don't be misled. Don't stop at this point and go on and on with it, forgetting all the rest. That is a mistake which many salesmen make, and it costs them a lot of orders.

You must go through the whole sequence from beginning to end, but when you have found a basic need, or you have the idea that the prospect is reacting to one of your main sales points—then keep on with it. Every time you add a sales feature to your story, couple it with the point which has aroused interest. Every sale, when it is made, fills a basic want on the part of the prospect. So, as soon as you have found out what that want is, stick to it and never let him forget it until you have the order.

THERE'S ALWAYS A MAIN SELLING ANGLE—FIND IT.

HOW SHE WARBLES!

When Aunt Aggie is asked to sing, generally the request is made as a favour to her—not to the audience. If Aunt Aggie, however, were a professional entertainer, then we shouldn't mind sitting back and listening. We should know that we would, at least, get reasonable entertainment.

The amateur boxer is good, but put him in the ring with a professional and it's highly doubtful whether he could last a round. When an amateur fighter turns professional he generally meets weak opposition before he's ready to come up against any really crack man.

There is a vast difference between amateurs and professionals. Because one man is dependent upon his success and his income by his efforts, he does his very best to give a good performance on every occasion.

There is just as big a difference between the amateur salesman and the professional salesman. The amateur is the man who thinks selling is an adventure and a way to earn money quickly. He takes up selling, doesn't prepare himself for his job, and wonders why he doesn't succeed.

Somebody said the other day that selling was an overcrowded profession, and then went on to remark, "Overcrowded by men who shouldn't really be salesmen at all."

The worst offenders in this respect are the men who have been selling for a few years. They often think they know it all, and don't try to prepare themselves for a higher income by studying their job more, by trying out new ideas, by altering their sales sequence.

If you want to be a professional salesman you have to study your job the whole time. You have to rehearse your part continually to make certain that you are perfect.

You may think this is going too far, but Arthur Hobart—one of the most successful salesmen of our time and now the managing director of a world-wide organisation—is quite prepared to tell anyone that when he was on the road he spent every Sunday rehearsing his sales sequence. His wife said that she knew his part as well as he did. But he says that those rehearsals helped him to success.

Are you prepared to do that? Do you want to be a professional salesman? If so, then act as a professional should.

HOW BORING!

The Club Bore was at it again. A music teacher living in the district had been knocked down by a car. I didn't hear the whole story, but it started something like this:

"Did you hear about Mrs. Bingham's accident? You know Mrs. Bingham, of course, don't you? She teaches music, and I believe she does extremely well. One of her pupils was—er— that girl, what's her name, Hilda something-or-other—I know her father—we were playing polo once when . . ."

And so he goes on and on. Eventually we were going to hear about the accident, but before we did hear about it we were to hear a lot of other things as well.

Too many salesmen are boring. They keep jumping from one thing to another—often telling a story which is of no interest to anyone except themselves.

You must, at every call, give a full sales sequence. But keep it brief. Every salesman should tell his story in as few words as possible.

WHERE'S HIS POCKET BOOK?

I saw a very good demonstration at a sales meeting. The platform was arranged to look as though it were a managing director's office. On to the stage came the assistant sales manager, trying to look like the managing director, and he took his place at a desk. Then a salesman was brought in to try to sell him a broadcast system for the factory—an installation to broadcast music while the workers worked.

The salesman went through quite a good sales story, proving that contented workers could produce more goods, output would grow, profits increase, and so on. When the sale was over, the sales manager asked the audience to comment on the sale. He didn't get the comment he wanted, so he said, "Now I'm going to show you where the salesman made a mistake."

He then took out of his pocket a tape measure, asked the pseudo-managing director to stand up, measured first the distance from the managing director's head to his pocket book just inside his jacket, and then the distance from his heart to his pocket book.

Turning to the audience he said, "I hope that demonstration proves something to you. The distance from a prospect's *head* to his pocket book is far greater than the distance from his *heart* to his pocket book. He will often spend money if the appeal is to his heart rather than to his head, and the salesman did not stress at all how much the workers would look up to him as an enlightened chief, how much they would appreciate what he was doing, and how happy they would be to work for such a man. Remember," he added, "appeal to the head by all means; a business man wants facts—but never forget, also, to appeal to the heart."

MAKE HEART APPEAL A PART OF YOUR SALES APPEAL.

THE TOWER OF BABEL

The Tower of Babel was never built because those working on its construction spoke different languages, and they couldn't understand each other.

I was reminded of this the other day when a shopkeeper called to see me. He is a grocer and a member of what we call our 'research group'. This consists of a number of shopkeepers who try to co-operate with us by giving us their side of the picture regarding salesmen.

"Mr. Tack," he said, "do you know what I said to a salesman who called upon me yesterday?"

"No."

"I asked him whether he was speaking Polish. He looked at

me in amazement—I think he thought I'd gone crackers. He said, 'I don't understand', so I asked him again, 'Are you talking to me in Polish? If so, I shouldn't continue because I don't understand Polish. Neither, for that matter, do I understand Dutch or Greek!' The salesman was still looking very amazed, so I said to him, 'Now, look here, young man. You've come into my shop to sell me scourers. That's fair enough—I stock scourers. But you're telling me that I shall sell them by the thousand. You expect me to give you an order far beyond my means. In other words, we're just not talking the same language.' The young man apologised, but I told him that he need not be sorry, I was just trying to help him. Then I went on to explain to him that many of the salesmen who called to see me didn't talk my language. They were thinking in terms of cash far beyond my means. Or else they were talking in coppers, and I couldn't be bothered—that wasn't my language either."

My friend concluded, "Teach your salesmen to talk the customers' language."

There is sound advice in that grocer's comments. Always be sure that you are talking in terms the other man will understand. Don't talk over his head, nor yet in figures below his buying capacity. Find something out about his trade before you call. If you can do this by judicious questioning, you can get an idea of his buying capacity. This applies to salesmen selling staples. The speciality man can always start high and work down if necessary.

TALK THE PROSPECT'S LANGUAGE.

FIFTEEN WAYS OF CREATING INTEREST IN YOUR PRODUCTS

If you can't make a prospect or buyer interested in the product you are selling then he will never place an order with you. To arouse his interest you have to explain to him continuously the benefits he will receive from placing an order with you.

You must, therefore, work out the greatest number of benefits that your goods or products will bring to the prospect. To do that you must, of course, know the reasons why your prospect will place an order with you. The average salesman believes that in the main his customers will only buy from him if they can make some money out of the deal.

That is very true for retailers who are buying day-to-day goods for their shops, which they must re-sell at a profit. But it isn't the whole story. I know the buyer of a small dress shop who regularly buys model dresses which she knows she will never be able to sell at anything like the price she pays for them. She buys them, however, from time to time because, as she says, it gives the shop prestige when she puts these dresses in her window. I remember a shopkeeper who became very annoyed because one of his competitors put a good line in his windows and obviously did well with that line. This shopkeeper placed a very much bigger order than he should have done for similar supplies, and stocked the whole of his window with these goods, just to show that he could do something better than his competitor.

He really placed his order (a) because his pride was hurt; and (b) because he was a little envious of the results achieved by his competitor.

Sometimes we buy to satisfy our sense of caution. For example, a salesman told me that when selling dictating machines he often hints at the fact that if the buyer's secretary were to be taken ill, or should leave him for some reason, it might be some time before she could be replaced. In this case, the dictating machine would take all his work, and any member of the staff could help him out by typing his correspondence until the gap was filled. The same salesman told me that he invariably told his prospect that he was running the risk of a cold when a typist came into the office and sneezed all over him. How much better to use the machine when members of the staff might have an attack of influenza coming on, or even an ordinary cold.

So far as fear is concerned, obviously fire extinguishers can be sold on the basis that if they are not bought the result might be loss of business, or even death. . . .

Here are some of the main reasons why people place orders:

1. Gain of money.
2. Caution.
3. Utility value.
4. To satisfy pride.
5. Sentiment.
6. Pleasure.
7. Benefits to health.
8. To satisfy hunger.
9. Because they are envious.
10. Because of love.
11. The need of self-preservation.
12. Because they want approval.
13. To make them feel important.
14. Because of security.
15. To give them more leisure.

Now it doesn't matter what you are selling, take each one of these points and try to line them up with your goods. Try to evolve your selling sentences around as many of these points as possible. If you can cover the whole fifteen you have the perfect sales presentation. But that is rarely possible. However, if you can cover seven of them you have built up a very good sales story, and you know that you will be able to hold the interest of your prospect all the time you are making the sale.

FOUR WAYS OF CREATING THE DESIRE TO BUY

From the beginning of the Approach to the Close of the order a salesman obviously does his best to Create the Desire to buy. The perfect sale is not when the salesman sells his goods, but when the prospect WANTS TO BUY THEM. And that can only be achieved when the salesman has, in fact, CREATED THE DESIRE on the part of the prospect to place the order.

The time, however, when a salesman must create the desire more than ever is just before he is going to attempt to close the order. Here are a few of the methods which can be used:

1. Tell a story of other customers who have purchased and have been happy at having placed their order.

2. Let the buyer glance at other orders in your order book, to show that if he doesn't place his order he will be behind his competitors.

3. Although you will maintain your enthusiasm high during the whole of the sale, become just that little bit more enthusiastic before the Close.

4. Put some positive suggestions to the prospect which will make him realise once more the benefits he will receive from buying from you.

ALWAYS EVOLVE PERFECT SELLING SENTENCES WHICH WILL CREATE THE DESIRE TO BUY.

CHAPTER VI

Fifty Ways of Improving Your Approach

It has been said time and time again that unless a salesman makes a good approach he cannot possibly arrive at a satisfactory close. The approach is all-important because, even if we don't believe in love at first sight, we do know that often we like or dislike somebody at the moment of meeting them. A salesman wants to be welcome always, and for that reason he should give careful thought to the type of approach he intends to use.

FIVE WAYS OF HOLDING ATTENTION AT THE APPROACH

1. Concentrate on one line or idea, irrespective of how many brilliant ideas you may have or how many lines you carry.
2. When entering a room, make quite certain that the door does not slam behind you, as this can be most disconcerting when making an approach.
3. If a buyer ignores you, don't try to make your approach. Stand near to him until he gives you his attention, which he will do provided you keep quiet.
4. Hold your head high when making your approach. This will give you more confidence, and will prevent you developing that hang-dog look which always conveys the impression that a salesman does not expect to get an order.
5. The simplest approaches are always the best. Remember that the vital step, creation of interest, follows the approach. Your appearance and attitude, therefore, count for almost as much at the approach as what you actually say.

THE FIVE SENSES

When making an approach always remember the five senses —sight, touch, taste, smell, and hearing. If, by demonstration, or by showing a sample, you can cover all the prospect's five senses, then you will make a very good approach. But in any event try to appeal to as many of them as you can.

The prospect's sight would be attracted by a well-designed leaflet or package; sense of touch by beautiful materials; a perfume could influence a buyer more quickly through his sense of smell than by a verbal description; if you sell foodstuffs, bear in mind the sense of taste; and, finally, you will only appeal to the prospect's sense of hearing if you have thought out in advance the perfect opening sentence.

THIRTEEN DO'S AND DON'TS FOR THE APPROACH

DON'T shake hands with someone you have never met before unless that person offers to shake hands with you first. Some prospects dislike shaking hands with every salesman who calls upon them. If you do shake hands, however, DO SO IN A PROPER MANNER.

DON'T show off as a strong man, by trying to break the prospect's arm with a terrific wrench.

DON'T be too friendly and, as you shake hands with him, clasp him with your other hand on his arm. The 'big-shot' salesman sometimes does this, but it is NEVER appreciated.

DON'T shake his hand as if you were working a pump. He doesn't want his arm to be flipped up and down in rapid succession.

DON'T give him a 'flannel' handshake—you know what a limp flannel feels like? Well then, you know what I mean! That sort of handshake takes all the enthusiasm out of your approach.

DON'T shake hands at all if your hands happen to be clammy.

DON'T try to wipe the clamminess off your hands on to your handkerchief as you walk up to your prospect.

DO clasp the prospect's hand firmly, give ONE SHAKE, and leave it at that.

After the handshaking business is over :

DON'T sit down unless you are invited to do so.

DON'T remove your coat unless you are invited to do so. The best plan is to take off your coat before entering the room.

DON'T park your bag in a spot where it could cause inconvenience to customers.

THE RIGHT WAY TO MAKE THE APPROACH

The approach is ALL IMPORTANT, and yet few salesmen analyse that part of their sale. They will spend hours working out why they didn't close an order, and yet overlook the main reason—that they didn't make a good approach.

I remember Harry. . . . He thought himself quite a good salesman, but he had what I call a 'SLOUCH APPROACH'.

He used to walk up to the prospect as if he were going to suggest some kind of crooked transaction. Yet Harry was quite an honest man. THAT KIND OF APPROACH LOST HIM A GOOD MANY ORDERS.

NEVER SLOUCH.

Then there was Allen. Allen was a 'big shot'—at least, he thought he was. At one time he was very immaculate, although he didn't look that way the last time I saw him.

He used the 'ARROGANT APPROACH'. Obviously, he wanted to show how important he was, but all he did was irritate the other man.

Then there was William. William always reminded me of the husband who goes shopping with his wife. You know the kind of fellow—walks a few steps into the underwear department, then hesitates, shuffles a few more steps along, then stops as if he ought not to be there at all.

His was the 'HESITANT APPROACH'. Quite the wrong way to meet the prospective buyer.

The Right Approach

Never slouch, never be arrogant, never hesitate. When you walk in to see a prospective buyer, put your shoulders back, hold your head high, have a smile on your face, and walk briskly towards him AS IF YOU WERE REALLY PLEASED TO MEET HIM. Remember, you are there to DO HIM A GOOD TURN.

If you were visiting a friend and you were going to do him that good turn you wouldn't slouch in, or hesitate. You would be EAGER to tell your friend about his good fortune.

MAKE YOUR PROSPECT FEEL THAT YOU ARE WORTH SEEING, BY MAKING THE RIGHT TYPE OF APPROACH.

PUT NEWS INTO THE APPROACH

Our country's changeable weather has become a salesman's best friend. H. R. Welks, a sales consultant, recently issued a report in which he stated that on checking up on one hundred approaches there were sixty-four occasions on which the salesman mentioned the weather while making his approach.

Practically every salesman, at some time or another, has walked into a shop or office, and his approach sentence has been, "Good morning, Mr. Jones, what a day! It couldn't be worse, could it?"—and has gone on with his standard approach. Sometimes it is wiser, however, to use news to combine with your approach, rather than the weather.

Try to avoid bad news, unless you happen to be selling something like fire extinguishers, when you might have to refer to a fire which has taken place in the vicinity. But watch out when you are reading your newspapers to see if there is any news item which you can link up with the product you are selling, and then try to bring that news item into your approach.

THAT 'NEWS' APPROACH CAN GET YOU OFF TO A GOOD START.

APPROACH BY LETTER

"Good morning, sir, here is my card."

This would be the worst type of approach, yet handing over a letter of introduction instead of a card can be an excellent beginning to a sale.

For many years I was quite against this form of approach, until one day somebody came to see me and handed me a letter from a personal friend. I read the letter through. It introduced the salesman who was calling, and told me that my friend thought that the salesman would be of service to me.

I was rather grateful to my friend for thinking of me, and I must say I warmed to the salesman slightly. Then he began selling in his normal manner, and he got an order.

It was then I realised that this form of approach could be quite helpful. Obviously, it doesn't apply to many businesses, but it does help a salesman when calling on executives.

If you are dealing with a customer you've known for years, and he recommends you to call upon somebody he knows quite well, then ask him if he would mind dropping his friend a line to introduce you. He'll probably be only too glad to do this, and you can take the letter along.

The letter approach is useful, although it must not be overworked.

WHAT GIVES YOU PLEASURE?

Think right now about yourself. Think of something that has given you pleasure. Perhaps your daughter has just passed an examination at school. Possibly you are going to take a girl friend to a show. Maybe you've won some sporting event.

Well, now, if a comparative stranger were to walk up to you and start off by saying, "Good morning, I was very pleased to hear how successful you were at the sports on Saturday", you would react favourably towards him, wouldn't you?

In selling, of course, you always have to talk in terms of the customer's interest, but what so many salesmen overlook is that they should do this from the moment they make their approach. Obviously they can't do this unless they can find out something about his interests, or his business. A salesman selling staple goods should know a great deal about his customers, so he is well placed. The speciality salesman making cold canvass calls, however, is often not in the position to know very much about his prospects in advance.

But he should try to find something out about them before selling. He can, by making inquiries from neighbours, receptionists, office boys, commissionaires, find out something about the business of the man he is going to see. Only the other day a salesman told me that he had obtained a very large order because, while waiting to see the managing director of a firm, he had questioned the receptionist about her chief, and found out that he had just won a prize in a flower show. Soon after he had made his approach he congratulated the managing director on winning the award. The managing director didn't cross-examine him as to how he had found out. He assumed that the salesman had also been to the flower show, and he talked flowers for quite a time.

The salesman is quite certain that this little piece of advance information had helped him to get the order.

So remember, before you make any call try to find out something about the person you are going to see. Listening to other salesmen can often help a lot.

MIXTURES DON'T PAY

During the war he escaped from Poland, reached England, joined the R.A.F., won a decoration, and was badly wounded.

When the war was over he stayed in this country, and started a small business with a friend. The friend soon relieved him of all his money, the business closed up, and the airman from Poland was completely broke. Then he was taken seriously ill.

When he recovered he couldn't find a job, but he managed to get a pedlar's licence. He bought some brushes, combs and odds and ends, and sold them from door to door. He wrote to me and asked for my help. He came to see me and told me that, despite the fact that he was working very hard, he was barely earning a living.

I asked him to demonstrate his approach to me. He opened his bag and showed me the mixture—brushes, combs, hair clips, and all that kind of thing, told me that they were all good value, and so on.

"That," I suggested, "is where you are making a mistake. People cannot grasp quickly the value of a range of articles. What you have to do each day is to pick out from the goods one article of special appeal—something that you think is better value than the others, and make your approach on that one article."

Some time afterwards he called to see me again, and told me that the 'one article' approach which he had tried was working very successfully. His business was prospering, and he now employed another man who was canvassing other streets with his goods. Recently, I heard that he has an office and is employing ten salesmen.

That man got on his feet by his own tremendous courage, but maybe the 'approach' helped him a little.

When making an approach, only deal with one point of your sales talk, or with one article, if you are selling a range of articles.

A 'FAX' APPROACH

We used to greet him with "Hello, Faxie", when we saw him coming towards us. He was a man of over sixty, who had been selling for about forty years. He didn't appreciate our greeting, and now I sometimes feel a little guilty that I used it, but when you're young you are rather apt to make mistakes in human relations.

We called him Faxie because whenever we got around to talking about salesmanship he would butt in with, "It's fax that count, my boy—fax!" That was how he pronounced the word f-a-c-t-s.

Those were the days when we were all somewhat impressed with high-pressure methods. Faxie was wiser than we were at that time.

The buyer does appreciate facts, and he often appreciates it when one is given in the approach. Here is a type of approach which brings forward an interesting fact:

"Mr. Brown, do you know that three thousand, two hundred people pass your door within two hours every morning?"

Or, "Mr. Biggs, careful people are just as prone to accidents as careless people."

Or, "More money will be spent on advertising soap next week than any other commodity. . . ."

Make your approach interesting with facts.

THE "HOW ARE YOU" APPROACH

I read a book written for the benefit of foreigners visiting this country. It stated that the standard greeting is usually, "How are you?" or "How do you do?"

The writer of the book told the reader that, although he must always use this form of greeting, he should never expect an answer. And if anyone greeted him in this manner he should never give an answer. Nobody really wants to know how the other person is.

In selling, however, the "How are you?" approach really does mean something. This type of approach is always a good weapon in the hands of a strong salesman, but I don't advise its use in the hands of a beginner.

A customer can always sense when a salesman is nervous. I remember hearing quite a timid salesman who was taught to use a question approach, saying to a prospect, "Could you use another fifty pounds a day profit from your business?"

The shopkeeper answered jocularly, "No, it wouldn't be the slightest use to me. I've just been left a million pounds."

That shattered the salesman. The strong salesman, however,

could have used exactly the same words, and the shopkeeper wouldn't have answered in that leg-pulling manner. He would probably have said, "Why, of course I could! What are you selling?"

The question approach, therefore, can be a very good approach.

"Mr. Jones, would you be interested in reducing your costs by 10 per cent?"

Or, "Would you like to make an extra pound an hour out of a weighing machine, without any capital outlay?"

Whatever approach you are now using, try to work out a question approach. It could bring you more orders.

MAKE HIM CURIOUS

Have you ever been in a train when somebody sitting next to you opened a case? And did you try to peep into that case? Have you ever been in an hotel lounge, sitting next to somebody who has suddenly taken out a pen and paper, written a few words on the paper, and looked at it? Didn't you wish you could see what he had written?

If we are prepared to admit our faults, many of us will say that we are extremely curious. Of course, that isn't really a fault at all except, perhaps, that it is not exactly ethical to try to look into somebody else's attaché case. Generally, however, curiosity is a very useful attribute.

It is because of this that the Curiosity Approach is such a good approach. For example, a salesman might have a wonderful guarantee with his product. He could produce that guarantee, show the blank side of it, and his approach could easily be, "Good morning, Mr. Johnson. Just look at this sheet of paper. Do you know it could be worth a thousand pounds or more to you?" Or a metal plate for an addressing machine—"Mr. Brown, a little piece of metal like this can save you hundreds of pounds a year."

And so on. Arouse curiosity, and you've made a good approach.

THE GIFT APPROACH

It's the old story of the sprat to catch a mackerel. I have had many hard-headed business men tell me that the offering of a gift in any way, shape or form, is never good trading. That it would never make them place an order. . . . Then I have seen these same men glow appreciably as an elaborate blotting pad arrives as a free gift from a firm with whom they have been trading.

Yes, they like their Christmas presents all right. They appreciate getting them. Most people like getting something for nothing, and when they do receive a free gift they don't stop to analyse the reason for the gift.

The gift approach is not used when calling on business houses; it is more often used when selling to householders.

When a salesman sells from door to door, the gift approach can be quite effective. "I would like you to accept this small brush, madam. Try it, and I shall call back to-morrow for your opinion."

The following day the salesman calls back, and he will probably get the opinion and an order for some other of his products.

The gift approach can often be used successfully.

THE SERVICE APPROACH

Here is one way a man built up a good business within about four years. He doesn't mind my telling you his story, but he did ask me not to print his name, so I'll just call him Joe.

Joe came out of the army with a great deal of mechanical knowledge and very little business ability. He got a job as a service engineer, servicing electrical equipment.

One day he was doing some work in a shop when the cash register went wrong. Joe had a look at it and put it right.

He thought about this, and then decided to call upon one or

two other shopkeepers in the district and ask them if he could check up on their cash registers. They didn't object. He looked them over, and now and again he found something wrong, and asked if he could do the repairs for them. Then he started buying one or two second-hand cash registers. After that, whenever he called upon a shopkeeper to look at his machine he would tell him that in his opinion he would be far better off with a recon-ditioned model than to go to the trouble of having his own machine overhauled. Often the shopkeeper would give him the order.

Joe now has several branches and is doing well. The service approach is a good one, if you are able to offer good service. The approach must be an honest one. The dentist who kept on taking out good teeth so that he could earn more money making false ones would soon find himself struck off the register. The salesman who told a phoney story about a machine being no good, just to sell the prospect a new one, wouldn't be on the right road to building up a successful business.

As Joe put it, "I never told a customer or prospect that he'd do well to buy an overhauled or new machine unless I felt that I was doing him a good turn by making that suggestion."

Bear that in mind when making the Service Approach.

DON'T BE A PASSER-BY

Practically every day I learn something new about selling. A little while ago I was in the market for recording machines. I had been thinking about buying for several months. I had mentioned this fact to quite a few people, and was enjoying the sensation of thinking around the subject, realising that possibly I was going to buy one day, although I didn't quite know when.

Most of us, when we are getting ready to buy, are a little like that. We are quite willing to spend our money on inexpensive everyday articles, but whenever we have to think of a large outlay we very rarely rush to buy. We keep thinking things over.

During the time that I was thinking about making this

purchase, a salesman called to see me. Obviously he had been tipped off by someone that I was in the market, and he felt he had only to call to get the order.

This is the approach the salesman made to me:

"Good morning, Mr. Tack. I happened to be passing by your building, and as I heard that you are interested in dictating machines I thought I'd look you up."

My whole interest evaporated as he made that approach. It was so lukewarm, so half-hearted that I felt I didn't want to hear very much more about his products.

I did let him go on—but I didn't buy. I bought a week or two later from another firm.

The whole point is that people are not interested in passers-by. They are not interested in salesmen who pop in on the off-chance of doing business.

All salesmen are given leads on occasion, and they should follow them up quickly. The very fact that they've been given a lead means that the prospect is enthusiastic about a certain type of product. Don't spoil his enthusiasm by a half-hearted approach. Far better to make a strong, enthusiastic approach.

"Good morning, sir. When I heard that you were interested in a recording machine I wasted no time. I came straight over to you, because I know that you will want to buy the best, and that's the type of machine that we manufacture. . . ."

Do you get the idea? Don't be a passer-by. Be a real salesman. Go out and SELL.

THE CONCENTRATION APPROACH

An approach which stresses the advantages of one particular item in the range of goods you are selling is always a good approach.

A little while ago I was making a journey to the North of England. Most of my fellow travelling companions had visited the bookstall on the station and bought newspapers or magazines to read on the journey. While we were awaiting the departure of the train, a newspaper boy marched past and, in a dreary voice, called out, "Papers, magazines, books . . ." Nobody stopped him to buy a paper.

A few minutes afterwards another boy came along. He was calling out, "Buy the latest Reader's Digest. Guaranteed to outlast your journey. . . ." He shouted out the same thing at every carriage, and when he stopped at ours two of the occupants bought the Reader's Digest, and others bought various magazines or papers from him as well.

That is a very good example of the strong approach with the one-action appeal.

YOUR NAME IS BEST

Everything is on a big scale in Chicago, so it didn't surprise me very much when the sales manager of a firm selling home appliances showed me the visiting card he had designed for his salesmen. It was about twelve inches square, and printed on it was a notice to the effect that the housewife could get bigger and better washes by buying their machine, and the retailer who bought the appliances to sell to the housewives could make bigger and better profits.

Another card I saw was a pictorial effort. It introduced the salesman with what I thought was rather a weak joke. I can't imagine a managing director in this country reacting favourably to the salesman who, first thing in the morning, sent in a card with a funny story on it.

I think that money spent on business cards for salesmen is usually a waste of money and time, whether they are of a standard type or have some special sales appeal.

Salesmen selling staple goods often have to have cards to send through to buyers, but I know many top-grade men in this field who have never carried a card; they give their name verbally.

A card for a speciality salesman is completely useless. Few buyers will see a speciality salesman who sends through a card. The answer is usually, "Not to-day!"

The rule should be, therefore, WHENEVER POSSIBLE DO WITH-OUT A CARD. If you are using cards now, then leave them all at home for a couple of weeks, and see what happens. You'll find that you won't miss the cards, the prospect won't miss the cards, and you may see more people by using just your name.

SIX GOLDEN RULES FOR MAKING THE APPROACH

Here are some golden rules to remember when making an approach:

1. Never gabble, always speak slowly, so that the prospect can hear every word.
2. Make certain that you have the best possible opening sentence. If you call regularly on your customers, never use hackneyed phrases such as '*How are things*' or '*Anything for me to-day?*' or similar phrases.
3. Avoid stunt approaches. You may arouse some momentary interest by putting over a stunt, but you will then be faced with a strong adverse reaction.
4. Always remember the five senses—sight, touch, taste, smell and hearing. Try to appeal at the approach to as many of these senses as possible.
5. If you can use a demonstration approach, do so, but never begin to demonstrate until you have sold the prospect to a certain extent on what you are selling, so that you arouse sufficient interest for him to want to see the demonstration.
6. A reference approach is always good. For example, when you can tell the prospect that a friend of his has recommended you to call.

MAKE A GOOD APPROACH, AND YOU ARE WELL ON YOUR WAY TOWARDS THE SALE.

CHAPTER VII

How to Make People Want to Buy From You

In years gone by, the advice of a sales manager to a new recruit was, "You've got to sell yourself before you sell your goods."

Now, we call this human relations. It comes to the same thing—a salesman has to make people want to buy from him.

WHAT IS A FAVOUR?

Stephen Kelly, now managing director of a firm manufacturing component parts for motor cars, started selling at the same time as I did. Someone asked me to give the reasons for his success. I answered, "He always did the hard favours."

My questioner said, "I don't understand you, what do you mean?"

I replied, "Most of us are only willing to do the little favours. For example, if somebody asks us to post a letter and we are going past the letter-box then, of course, we do it. But if we have to walk two miles out of our way to do it, then the majority of us make excuses."

Many salesmen do favours for their customers.

"I'll send you a catalogue"—and a catalogue is sent.

"I'll arrange for our expert to give you advice on window-dressing"—and the arrangement is made.

It hasn't cost the salesman much in time or trouble—and certainly nothing in money.

Kelly did all the little favours for his customers, but he did the hard favours as well. I remember one customer was having trouble over shortage of staff, and Kelly helped him on Sunday to unpack crates. I recollect Kelly lending his car to another customer who had to take his wife to a South Coast resort. She hadn't been too well, the customer had only a small business, and he hadn't much money. Kelly loaned his car, and Kelly walked that week. Walked, and bussed, and trained all at his own expense.

You should remember Kelly's example. Anyone can carry out the little favours. It's only the exceptional man who does 'hard' favours.

OBSERVATION

Have you ever played a game called OBSERVATION? Somebody puts a dozen or more articles on a tray, which is then covered with a cloth. It is uncovered for you to inspect the articles on the tray for perhaps two minutes, when it is again covered; then you have to try to enumerate as many articles as you possibly can. Others in the party do the same thing, and the winner is the person who has noticed most objects.

It's good fun, but you don't get paid for it. If you put as much effort into your daily work as a salesman as you do when taking part in such games, you would increase your sales.

The salesman must be on the look-out all the time for leads to help his sale along—leads which will enable him to sell himself more effectively to the prospect.

Recently, we carried out a test with fifty salesmen. Some of these men called to see me, others were calling upon executives of our company. We found out from each executive what his favourite hobby was, and then took action. In one corner of my office, in full view of any visitors, I placed a set of golf clubs. In the office of one of my managers we put a silver cup which he had won running for the Blackheath Harriers some years before. In another office, that of an executive who was very fond of riding, we had a large photograph of a pony in a field. . . .

Now here is something for you to think about. Out of some fifty salesmen who called to see us, only three mentioned the articles which had been put in the rooms to test their powers of observation.

What wonderful opportunities there were in each case for the salesman to sell himself quickly by talking of a subject which obviously interested the person he had come to interview.

A salesman must be as observant as a detective, because what he sees will often give him a clue to an order, or enable him to talk in terms of the prospect's interest.

DON'T BE TOO BRILLIANT

James Barnes is certainly one of the most brilliant all-round men I have ever met. At Oxford he took his B.Sc. with the greatest of ease. Then he decided that he wouldn't become a schoolmaster after all, and he joined a clothing manufacturer.

He started with the firm in a clerical position in the sales department, but soon became so popular that when a vacancy occurred for another man on the road, he was chosen.

He is a scratch golfer, a first-rate cricketer, and plays a sound game of tennis. He can fish with the best, and is a great lover of botany.

One day we had lunch together. He told me that he was as busy as ever, and I answered, "It's easy enough for you! You don't have to sell your goods; anyone would be willing to listen to you talk on practically any subject."

He grinned and said, "When I first started selling I always brought the conversation round as quickly as I could to one of my pet subjects, because I wanted to swank and to show the buyer that he was dealing with someone of importance. But I found that it didn't go over too well. One day I was having a chat with a buyer who told me that he had spent the week-end playing golf. I asked him what his handicap was, and he told. me fourteen. Then he asked if I played golf. On learning that I did, he asked me what my handicap was, and I told him that I wasn't good enough to have a handicap. Straight away he started demonstrating to me how I could improve my swing, my stance and everything else. After the demonstration I got an order—and a good one, at that.

"That taught me a lesson that I've always remembered—a salesman should never appear to be cleverer than the buyer."

ASK HIS ADVICE

Have you noticed the way friends always seem pleased when you call on them for advice?

A new recruit to salesmanship obtained a position with a firm selling men's hosiery. He was conscious of his age, but tried to overcome it by brilliant selling methods. They didn't get him very far.

One day he visited his head office. He said to his sales manager, "I think you ought to sack me. When I call on buyers I feel uncomfortable. I see the friendly way they greet some of their old friends in the trade. They never greet me like that. They don't seem to think I know anything about the business, although, as you know, I spent five years in the warehouse—probably longer than many of the old-timers ever did."

The sales manager said, kindly, "The majority of buyers have the feeling that a man who has just started selling doesn't know very much about his business, and that is why, although they are prepared to look at his samples, they are not prepared to listen to his advice. And if a salesman can't advise a buyer, then he has a difficult time selling. You can alter the whole situation by remembering that you are a newcomer to selling. Don't try to hide the fact. When you call upon a buyer, ask for his advice. Don't sell to him—let him sell to you. You'll see what a difference it makes."

The young man did just that. He is now an old-timer himself, but he is never tired of telling the new recruits to selling, "Don't show off; ask for advice and you'll get more orders."

GOODBYE FOR EVER

You probably know the words of the well-known song which includes quite a few goodbyes before the end actually comes.

As a salesman, always take your leave quickly—after one goodbye. The object of making the call was to make a sale. So soon as you have obtained the sale you are ready to depart. To hurry off might be ill-mannered, so a few friendly remarks to cement confidence are in order. But don't stay longer than that. Don't outstay your welcome. Don't be so grateful to your customer for giving you an order that you feel you must retail to him all the stories and yarns which you have heard from your fellow salesmen on the road.

Don't say goodbye, make for the door and then come back again with another suggestion. Make your goodbye snappy— but try not to say goodbye until you've got an order.

LET HIM DO YOU A FAVOUR

Brenda King was a charming girl. Whenever she started a new job all her associates liked her. She was always so willing to do anything for anyone. After a while, of course, other people did little things for her. When this happened, however, Brenda was never happy until she had done a much greater favour for the person who had done some little favour for her. If someone lent her a pencil, then a day or so afterwards she would have to buy six brand new pencils and hand them over with a *Look what I've done for you now* expression.

If anyone stayed five minutes late to help her, she wasn't happy until she had stayed late for an hour or more to help that person.

On the face of it she was too grateful for what was done for her. The fact was, however, that she looked upon favours as something deserving a kind of revenge.

There are quite a lot of people like that. A salesman should always be ready to help others, but he should remember that people like doing favours, and if a customer or prospect, or a friend, does you a small favour—be pleased to accept it. Don't start racking your mind to think what you can do to pay it back.

It pleases many people to grant favours.

TWELVE WAYS OF REMEMBERING A NAME

Remembering someone else's name is a major problem for most people. The reason? Generally speaking it is because we are not so interested in the other man that we want to remember his name.

I have read of many different methods of solving this problem. Association of ideas is one—remembering the person's name by associating it with something else.

After trying all systems, however, I found one the simplest. Repeat the name at least twelve times during an interview. Whenever you meet anybody, first of all make certain that you have his name correctly. If the introduction has been gabbled and you haven't been sure of the name, then ask for it to be repeated. Ask for it to be spelt, if necessary, but get that name right. Then make certain of using it at least a dozen times during the conversation.

The other man won't object, he likes to hear his own name, and you'll remember it for ever after.

BE SYMPATHETIC

I was at a party a little while ago where I overheard a married woman saying to a young woman of about twenty-seven, "My dear, you don't know how lucky you are to be single."

I suppose quite a few single women hear that remark, but they don't believe it. More often than not, it is said by someone who is happily married to give encouragement to a girl who is still single. Sometimes, of course, it is said vindictively.

I said to the recipient of the advice, "Does it worry you a little to hear that sort of thing?"

She answered, "Yes, it does make me a bit fed up." Then, quite unexpectedly, she added, "I'm terribly jealous of them really."

I said, "You need not be, you know."

Half our worries and troubles would be eased if only everyone would tell the truth. But, of course, there are many things about which we never do speak the truth, and marriage is usually one of them. Many a married woman is quite unhappy, although she would be the very last woman to tell a single person to remain unmarried. If she did, however, the single person could sympathise with her, and that might help her a little.

We all need a little sympathy at times, but we don't often get it. Sympathetic understanding of the other person's problems is a very useful asset to a salesman.

I remember a friend of mine who got quite a nice order from a West End store during the slump years. He called on a buyer, only to be greeted with, "Sorry, but the bar's been put up and I'm not allowed to spend any more money. They tell me my department's overstocked already."

Instead of my friend muttering something about bad luck and then walking off, he said, "I'm sorry for myself, because I can't get an order. But if you don't mind my saying so, I'm even more sorry for you. I think you must be in a most difficult position, with salesmen calling to see you all day long to sell you something, and you unable to buy even if the lines are goods which you require. Of course, I'm quite sure the people on top don't quite understand your problems—that you've got to keep buying, to shift some of the old stock."

That gave the buyer the opportunity he wanted to tell someone all his troubles. He talked to my friend on this subject for about half an hour. Then my friend got around to talking about some of his samples. The next thing that was happening was that the buyer was looking at his samples. Then my friend got an order—one of the biggest he had ever taken—for forward delivery.

A little sympathy had pulled off a big sale for him.

MY LIFE STORY

I learned this lesson from a young salesman who called to see me to sell me office equipment.

He was not making very good headway, when suddenly he said to me, "You know, Mr. Tack, you must have had a most interesting career. How did you actually start in business?"

I tried to look a little diffident, as we all do when we are asked for our life story. Then I told him everything that had happened to me from the age of about sixteen onwards.

After a while, he started his sales sequence. I had more or less made up my mind to give him an order, but decided that I would send him along first to see our office manager to discuss the question.

Parsons, the office manager, was disengaged, and I sent the young salesman along to him. After a few minutes I thought I would join them. As I arrived at Parsons' room, I was just going to walk in, when somebody stopped me to ask me a question, and while answering it, I couldn't help overhearing the voice of the young salesman. I heard him saying, "Mr. Parsons, you must have had a most interesting career, building your way up to be manager here. How did you start in business?"

I smiled to myself, turned round and walked back to my own office.

A little while later Parsons rang through to tell me that he thought the equipment was all right and that we should have it. I agreed. The equipment was worth purchasing if only because of the one lesson I had learned at that interview. THE WAY TO WIN OVER A MAN TO YOUR WAY OF THINKING IS TO LET HIM TALK ABOUT HIMSELF—AND ONE WAY TO DO IT IS TO ASK HIM HOW HE STARTED IN BUSINESS.

TEN WAYS OF BEING A GO-GIVER

For many years a salesman was referred to as a '*go-getter*'. This was supposed to describe a salesman fighting hard to get everything he could from his customer. No real salesman would like to be called a 'go-getter', because these words are the very opposite to the true meaning of salesmanship.

B. J. Evershed, managing director of Eversheds, the well-known suppliers of stationery and calendars, has a far better expression. He says that a salesman must be a '*go-giver*'. In other words, if you try to give a lot to your prospects and customers, you will get a lot in return. What can you give him?

1. You can give him a complete understanding of what you are selling.
2. You can give him politeness.
3. You can give him the benefit of your technical knowledge.
4. You can give him praise.
5. You can give him your attention when he wants to talk.
6. You can give him good service.
7. You can give him advice as to how he can sell more goods.
8. You can give him sympathy and understanding, if he is worried about anything.
9. You can give him inspiration.
10. You can give him friendship.

To be a successful salesman be a *go-giver*.

FIND OUT HIS NAME

"Good morning, Mr. Er—— Thank you for seeing me, Mr. Er—um—er—— Well, yes, sir, yes. No, Mr. Er—er."

All right, I admit that no salesman would make an approach like that. But whenever you don't use a man's own name you are not making a good approach.

If you are selling staple goods, then the chances are that you will have a list of your buyers or prospects, or you will know the names of the buyers you are to see.

If you're a speciality salesman working an area systematically then the way to find out names of prospects is to make use of every call you make, to discover this information.

"What's the name of the owner of the shop next door?"—a straightforward question which nobody minds answering.

Every time you make a call try to find out the name of the next person you are going to see.

MAN TO WOMAN

Last time I was in the U.S.A. I met Gladys Hart. She is well known over there as being one of the biggest carpet buyers in the world.

I said to her, "You probably see as many salesmen as any man, or woman for that matter. What tip would you give me that I can pass on to salesmen?"

She smiled, and it was a very sweet smile, as she said, "You know, there are many women buyers to-day, and not many men know how to sell to them. Here is the best advice I can give: the interviews with women should be placed on a man-to-man basis. Just tell them that!!"

Well, I'm telling you just that.

FOUR TIPS FOR AN 'OLD-TIMER'

Very early in my career I got a job selling umbrellas. The firm gave no sales training, neither did they have a sales manual. They sent me out for a week with their senior salesman, who was about to retire. He wasn't too helpful, until the time came when we were about to part company. I asked him then if he could give me any advice as to how I could be successful.

He answered, "The stuff's all right. The customers are all right. But you won't do any good unless you remember the four golden rules of selling."

I sat back and waited for some really good, helpful advice, but this is all he told me:

"You won't sell very much," he repeated, "unless you are liked. And it's very easy to be liked. All you have to remember is first to make everyone you meet feel important; next, give the other person credit for everything—it doesn't matter whether you thought of it first or not. The third rule: be tactful with everyone; and, lastly, laugh at yourself a lot."

At that time I was very disappointed in the advice given to me by the old-timer, but I have learned since that his advice was truly golden.

Make everyone you meet feel a little more important when you leave them than when you met them. Make the typist feel like a secretary. Make the clerk feel like an office manager.

Originate as much as you like. Think out as many ideas as you can, but when you're selling let the other man feel that the ideas are his. No one likes a man who is tactless. Make certain that you are tactful all the time.

And, finally, never mind telling a story against yourself. Everyone will like you just a little bit more for that.

DON'T BE A SMART ALEC

Have you ever seen this act on the stage? The scene is an office. The owner of the office is completely broke. Then suddenly a customer arrives, so the comedian who takes the part of the hard-up business proprietor gets to work to show how really busy he is.

As the visitor walks into his office he is busy answering a telephone, refusing an order for a thousand pounds' worth of this or ten thousand pounds' worth of that. He arranges for the 'phone to ring every few minutes, to enable him to complete mythical deals. When the visitor is seated he talks in millions, and of his great successes. And then, of course, in the end the visitor turns out to be the income tax collector.

It wouldn't be a bad thing if the income tax collector were always to walk in on these Smart-Alec conversations. Too many men like to appear over-clever. They like to tell you of the great business deals they have pulled off, sometimes by using a little trickery. Possibly they have never used that trickery, they may be absolutely honest men, but they think it is clever to appear smart.

Well, it isn't. Most of us are afraid of people who are too clever.

Never be a Smart-Alec.

DON'T SELL

I had spoken to a salesman about a customer who should have placed a very large order with him. He had been with that customer for over two hours; he had answered every objection in the correct manner; he had used all his sales points. . . . But he was honest enough to say to me, "The order has been put off because he wasn't going to be talked into an immediate decision. He wants to decide in his own time."

Some time later, I met the customer, who was a friend of mine. I told him about the interview I had had, and asked why he had not placed the order. In fact, the order had never been placed.

He answered : "Well, there was something about him that I didn't like. I would say that he lacked honest friendliness. He didn't give me the feeling that he was trying to help me. I gained the impression that he had one object in mind, and that was to sell to me."

Honest friendliness means not selling the whole time—not talking about your own products the whole time—*not talking too much*, and thinking more during the sale of the prospect than of yourself.

I HOPE THIS NEVER HAPPENS TO YOU

The action took place in a garage outside London. At the time I was selling specialised equipment for motor dealers. I made a fair approach, and went on talking, and talking, and talking. The prospect said very little. I became irritated with him, and began to recollect all that I had learned about dealing with a prospect who wouldn't talk. When I couldn't think of anything else to say I dried up.

Then the prospect said, in a broad North Country accent, "The trouble with you is you talk too much." He put an adjective in between the 'too' and the 'much'.

I don't think I ever felt more uncomfortable in my whole selling career.

The reason, of course, why I felt so bad about it was that I knew he was telling the truth, and we always feel a lot worse when we are criticised, and we know the criticism is justified.

Now this talking and listening business is most difficult to cure. In fact, I haven't found a cure for it. I've lectured about it at some length. I've written about it, and now I'm telling you about it. But I can chalk it up as one of my failures.

The reason is because so few prospects talk to salesmen as that garage proprietor talked to me. That is why the average man—yes, it doesn't matter whether he's a salesman or not, I'm talking about everyone now—talks far too much.

In private life it doesn't matter a great deal, but in selling it can prevent you from obtaining orders.

I remember a student taking our Course who had this failing. I didn't realise it until he called to see me. He had studied the lesson which dealt with this very subject, but it didn't stop him talking, and talking, and talking. I did my best to put him right.

He called again, a little later, to see one of my managers. My manager said to me afterwards, "What can we do to stop him talking?"

I could only answer, "Very little."

To get the best out of this book you should continually ask yourself the question, "Does this apply to me?"

If you said that right now, your immediate reaction would be, "Oh, no, I don't talk too much", because we always feel that we are so interesting to other people. We always think they like to hear us. But let me ask you this question: would you like to sit back and listen to someone talking to you for ten, fifteen or twenty minutes without a break, without your interrupting or saying anything?

You wouldn't? Here's a short cut to winning popularity, influencing people, getting your own way, getting yourself liked.

CUT DOWN YOUR TALKING TIME BY ABOUT 25 PER CENT.

When making a sale, see that you don't do more than sixty per cent of the talking. Let the prospect do the other forty per cent. And when he is talking—be a good listener. Be a sincere listener. Do actually listen to everything he says. Don't be thinking of what you are going to say next. Don't interrupt him. Don't jump in before he has finished a sentence and complete the sentence for him. Don't tell an anecdote to bear out his story.

Here's a lesson in itself: MAKE YOURSELF AN EXPERT LISTENER, AND TALK LESS. Confucius said, WHEN YOU LISTEN, YOU LEARN.

When a salesman learns to listen, he sells more.

MY FRIENDS ARE YOUR FRIENDS

Do you think it hypocritical to tell someone, for example, that your political views are Liberal when they are, in fact, Conservative or Labour? Do you think it hypocritical to tell a prospect that your greatest interest is in sketching, when the only time you put pencil to paper is to write down your orders?

If you do, then listen to the advice of Albert Reed, who is now the sales manager of a firm selling office appliances.

This is what he says:

"Everyone likes to feel that your interests are similar to theirs. If a customer or prospect is interested in fishing he likes to think that the man he is talking to is also interested in fishing. If his hobby is gardening, then he'll be happier if he's talking to a man who is also keen on this.

"I once heard a salesman say that he was everything the buyer was. If the buyer was a Communist, he was a Communist. If the buyer was an atheist, he was an atheist, and so on.

"I don't agree with that. That's going too far; it's no good pretending you are something you are not. But there's a much easier way out than that. It never pays to argue with a prospect and, anyway, a man is entitled to his own opinion. The best thing to do is just to listen and say nothing. If you do that, the prospect gains the idea that you are agreeing with him and that your interests are his interests. I've been with a prospect who spouted Spiritualism almost for hours. I'm no Spiritualist, but I didn't say anything. I just let him go on talking, and if he cared to think that my interest in listening was proof that I, too, was a Spiritualist—well, that was entirely up to him."

Thank you, Albert Reed, for good advice.

SELL THE ASSISTANTS

Bloggs walks into a shop, makes a good approach, sees the owner and delivers a first-class sales sequence. Bloggs is a good salesman—one of the best. He sells himself well, the prospects like him, sign a decent-sized order, shake him by the hand and tell him to come back next time he's in the district and they'll see what else they can do for him. Bloggs smiles, thanks the customers nicely for the order, and with a cheery wave of the hand at the assistants, he walks right out of the shops.

Bloggs has sold again. Yes, he's a good salesman all right. But he could be a lot better, because he overlooks one lesson— and it's a most important lesson.

The owners of the shops, unless they are one-man shops, don't sell all the goods they stock. Sales, in the main, are made by assistants, perhaps also by a manager.

The good salesman not only sells to the owner or buyer, he also sells his goods to the assistants. He takes time off to explain the benefits of his products, to become enthusiastic about them, so that the assistants not only like him, but they like the goods he sells as well.

If Bloggs had done that, when he called back to see the owner on his next visit he would not only have got an order, he would have got a very good order, because the assistants, knowing all about his products, would have sold the goods for him.

Help the assistants to sell your goods by winning their respect and friendship.

THANKS FOR THE DISPLAY

"That fellow's too big for his boots." A shopkeeper said this to one of his assistants after a salesman had left him.

Do you know the mistake the salesman had made? It wasn't that he had shown off. He hadn't swanked—he had just forgotten to say "Thank you". Some of his shoes had been displayed by the shopkeeper, who had made what he thought was an attractive card to help the display. He had looked forward to the salesman calling because he felt that the salesman would be pleased with the show. But the salesman hadn't commented at all.

Whenever a customer shows your goods in his window or on his counter, always remember to thank him.

EVERYONE LIKES THEM

Provided we're not in debt and are not, therefore, dreading the postman's knock, we all do like to receive letters.

I know a managing director of a company employing a thousand workers who, whenever he can, goes to the mailing department early in the mornings, and sorts out all the letters addressed to himself so that he can read them before his secretary.

If, then, we all do like to receive more letters, surely one way of getting more sales and better results must be to write more letters. Far too few salesmen go to the trouble of writing to their prospects or customers after visiting them. They all tell you they're too tired in the evening to do such a thing.

The men who reach the top have often had to work long hours—they've had to work when they've been so tired that they could hardly keep their eyes open. But they went on doing their job.

If others want to succeed, they must realise that, however tired they feel, they must do *their* job properly. Make a habit of writing to a prospect who doesn't sign the order. Drop him a line to thank him for the interview; tell him that you'll call again one day, and hope to be of service to him. Drop a line to your customers, just to tell them that you hope all is going well with them. When you see your own managing director or sales manager, drop him a line afterwards and thank him for the interview.

And here's another bit of advice that can be of great help to you. If ever you go for a job and you can't land it at the interview, write a letter immediately you return home, pointing out as strongly as you can how much you would like to work for that firm.

Don't rely on your company to do all your letter-writing for you. It's so easy to put on your report: *Write to so-and-so about this. Send details about such-and-such to X & Co.*, and so on. If you want to win the approval of your firm, and to get more business, you'll do more letter-writing yourself; not necessarily letters to get appointments or interviews—they're often worthless—but letters which will build up goodwill—letters which will make the other man say of you, "He's a nice chap. Whether he gets your business or not, he always drops you a line."

Keep sending those 'lines'—they can be worth a lot of money to you.

WHO GOES THERE—ENEMY OR FRIEND?

I was buying a shirt, and had just completed the deal when in walked a salesman. The owner of the shop introduced me to him. It was his brother-in-law.

I decided that I might be interested in a sports jacket, and another of the assistants started showing me these jackets while the brother-in-law began talking business with his relative.

I heard him say, "Yes, I should have a couple of boxes of

those." Then a little later, "No, don't touch them, they won't go at all." And later still, "This is something really special!"

After looking at several coats I decided not to buy, and I went back to the owner of the shop and said jokingly: "I hope you've given your brother-in-law a nice order."

"Oh, yes," he said, "I always do that."

Turning to the salesman, I said, "You certainly seem to be doing your brother-in-law a good turn from what I heard, anyway."

"Yes," he answered, "I always do that!"

"What about your other customers," I said. "Do you treat them all like this?"

"Good gracious, no!" he said. "I do it for Eric, but I wouldn't do it for everyone."

"Be careful," said Eric, the shop owner, "you know Mr. Tack is one of those sales experts."

I laughed. "Not at all," I said. "It's just that I'm very interested in selling."

"Go on," said Eric, "teach him something."

"I couldn't," I said. "Obviously he knows his trade much too well. But here's a tip I will give you," I said, turning to the brother-in-law. "Why don't you treat all your customers as you do your brother-in-law? If you did you would increase your business—not rapidly, it's true, but slowly, so that in a couple of years you would have a turnover far greater than you have to-day."

The salesman smiled. I don't think he believed me, but I was telling the truth.

EVERY SALESMAN, WHEN SELLING TO A CUSTOMER, SHOULD ACT AS IF HE WERE SELLING TO HIS BEST FRIEND.

SIX TIPS FROM A BUYER

As Victor Barnard buys for a group of chain stores, and spends five days a week seeing salesmen, he knows as much about selling as anyone. When asked what irritated him most about men who called to see him, he answered:

"Salesmen who lean on my desk.

"Men who let their eyes wander all over the papers on my desk, as if they were trying to seek some private information.

"Men who keep tipping back in their chairs.

"Men who will keep scratching a spot on their face.

"Men who talk too much.

And, worst of all, men who will try to impress me with their great importance."

So if you're one of the salesmen who has to call to see Mr. Barnard, you'll know what to avoid in the future.

CHAPTER VIII

How You Can Succeed Where Others Fail

H. S. WESTON, Sales Controller of Wm. P. Hartley Ltd., defines selling as 'one human mind influencing another human mind'. A salesman has to influence people so that they will buy from him in preference to buying from a competitor.

They buy for two reasons—the first, because they feel that they have a need for the product; the second, because they like the salesman who is selling it to them.

If a prospect dislikes a salesman he usually dislikes his goods. When he likes a salesman he usually likes his goods. And that is the way most men sell.

THIRTEEN CERTAIN WAYS OF INFLUENCING OTHER PEOPLE

There is no better way of assimilating knowledge than by letting the brain work to fathom things out for itself, so I am going to ask you to do a little work right now. I am going to tell you the story of a salesman's day, and in it I have listed thirteen mistakes in human relationship which have been made, either by him or by those with whom he has come into contact. I want you to try to discover these mistakes as you read through the story. If you haven't found the thirteen by the time you have completed it, don't continue, and read my explanation. Go back to the beginning and read it again—and keep on reading it, until you have discovered all the mistakes by yourself.

This lesson on human relationship can help you to succeed, PROVIDED that after studying these thirteen major points you continually check up on yourself to see that you don't fall into any of the errors that I have listed.

Check up after every interview. Check up after every meeting with a friend or a stranger. Make certain that you haven't made any of the mistakes that John Brown makes in this story.

HOW NOT TO WORK

"Come in," sang out Evans, sales manager of the XYZ Company.

Brown, about to knock again, heard the invitation and walked into his sales manager's office.

"I'm surprised to see you here," said Evans, as Brown took off his hat and coat and threw them on to a chair. "I thought you'd be out on your ground, selling. But sit down."

Brown sat down. "Well," he said, "I wanted to clear up one or two points with you, and I felt that it might be difficult to explain things in a letter. That's why I came along."

"You couldn't have chosen a worse morning," said Evans. "I'm snowed under with letters; I have a meeting in half an hour; and my doctor has just 'phoned to confirm that an X-ray taken of my tummy shows that I have a duodenal ulcer. And if that isn't enough for one morning," he added, with a grin, "you walk in!"

"I'm sorry," said Brown. "But I couldn't carry on with my work until I had one or two points out with you."

"Let's hear 'em then," said Evans. "What's troubling you?"

"Do you mind if I smoke?" asked Brown.

"No."

Brown took his cigarettes out of his pocket and offered the case to his manager.

"No, thank you," said Evans. "I'm afraid I shall have to cut out smoking and drinking."

"Do you mind if *I* smoke?" asked the salesman again.

"No, you carry on."

Brown lit up. "This is the point," he began, as the sales manager relaxed in his chair and looked expectantly at him. "I'm a blunt man and I believe in speaking straight from the shoulder. I'm not satisfied with the way things are going. You gave me my territory—you marked it out on a map for me. But I've found that part of that territory overlaps McLean's—he works next to me. That's a bad mistake to make, and it's caused me endless bother. And, then, another thing—you sent out a quotation for me the 'day before yesterday, and the customer was addressed as Marsden, when his name's Mansfield. . . ."

Evans let Brown go on with his criticisms. When he had finished, he said, "Is that the lot?"

"Well, yes, that's the lot," said Brown. "I know you don't mind my speaking plainly to you."

"No, I don't mind a bit," replied Evans. "I'm going to check up on these things right now."

The sales manager started pressing buzzers and ringing through on his intercommunicating telephone to accumulate the facts he required. He was soon able to point out to Brown that the reason for wrongly addressing the sales director to whom he had written on Brown's behalf was because Brown's writing was so bad, and he had not troubled to follow the company's rule to write all customers' names in block capitals. The typist had tried to decipher the name, but had made a mistake.

He also dealt with other queries, which were of little consequence.

Then he said, "The trouble with you is that you're not getting results and, because of that, you're trying to find excuses for yourself by saying that we're making all the mistakes here. Well, my lad, that's not the way to look at things, and that's not the way to get on."

"That isn't true!" Brown began to feel a little hot under the collar. "It's not true at all," he said. "You've always told us to see you when we had anything on our minds, and now, when I come along, you blame me for it."

Evans lost his temper completely. He told Brown what he thought of him. He also intimated that if he had any more of his nonsense he could find another job. That quietened Brown down, but after more discussion he said, "But what about this territory business?"

Evans again compared his master copy of territories with Brown's copy, and it was quite plain that a mistake had been made in outlining Brown's territory.

"That's just a question of plain common-sense," Evans said, as he pointed out that although the line wasn't strictly correct, Brown must have realised that something was wrong earlier, and he should have written in about it.

"Why should I?" asked Brown. "I was given the territory map, and I worked from it."

They went on discussing territories for quite a while. Finally, Evans said, "I have to go to a meeting now. Anyway, we've cleared the air and I hope everything is straightened out."

"Well, yes," said Brown. But he didn't mean it.

The two men shook hands and the sales manager slapped Brown on the back to try to make him feel that all was friendly again between them.

Leaving the building, Brown walked moodily down the road.

"What are you looking so cheerful about?"

Brown looked round and saw Jim Robinson, a typewriter salesman. "Hello, Jim," he said. "Just had a bust-up with the S.M. He thinks he's the greatest man in the world. Won't listen to anyone."

"Come on," said Jim. "Let's go and have some coffee to soothe your nerves."

The two men walked towards a coffee bar, and were soon drinking coffee. Brown felt much better as he got all his complaints off his chest.

"Heard about Rodgers?" said Robinson, as they lit cigarettes.

"No," said Brown, "what's happened to him?"

"You don't know? Why, he's got into trouble with that girl he's been taking about. He's a perfect . . ."

"He's that all right!"

They talked a little longer about Rodgers and then they left the teashop. Robinson walked towards his car, which was parked in a nearby street, and Brown caught a bus to enable him to make his first call of the day.

He slumped in the seat and stared moodily at the shops as the bus jolted its way along the road.

"Fares, please!" Brown didn't look round.

"Fares, please!" Brown came to with a start.

"A tenpenny."

The ticket was handed to him. He put it in his pocket, and once more stared out of the window. When he looked round again he noticed the conductor taking the fare from another passenger, and said, "Do you know where Woodville Road is?"

The conductor looked at him. "Yes."

"It's along Harringway, isn't it?"

Yes."

"About half-way down?"

"A bit more than that."

"Will you give me a call when we get there?"

"Yes."

Once more he turned to his occupation of looking at the shop windows. It was only after some little while that he realised that the bus had reached the end of Harringway. He jumped up, hurried towards the platform, and said to the conductor, "Didn't I ask you to give me a call?"

"I forgot."

Brown muttered something about bus drivers and conductors and all their families. The bus slowed down, and he jumped off.

He had to walk back half a mile, but eventually he arrived at his destination. Walking into the building, he pressed the buzzer at the reception office.

A fair, rather pretty girl put in an appearance, and asked him what he wanted. He told her his business. A short while afterwards a young man appeared and said to Brown, "I'm in the Accounts Department. Mr. Davies told me to have a word with you first."

Brown went into his sales talk and sold well. The young man from the Accounts Department, after letting him finish, told him to wait a few minutes. Obviously he went in to see the managing director, because he returned later and said, "Mr. Davies will see you. Will you come with me?"

Brown and the Accounts Department gentleman made their way into Mr. Davies' office. As they walked in, the managing director greeted them with, "Well, now, what is it you've got? What's it all about?"

Brown said, "I've been explaining to your clerk here . . ." and went on with his story once more.

"Do you think it's the sort of thing you want, Harrison?" said Davies, to the member of his Accounts Department.

"I did think so when I heard it briefly. I thought we could do with it then, but I don't think we ought to arrive at any hasty decision. We should get some other quotations."

"Yes, that would be a good idea," said Davies. "I think that's what we'll do."

But Brown didn't give up easily. He went on selling as hard as he could. He wanted to get the order on the spot. After a while, the managing director said, "Harrison, take Mr. Brown through to our Accounts Department. Let him look around, so that he can get a more accurate idea of what we require."

Brown's spirits rose. He felt he was getting near a sale as Harrison escorted him out of the office and upstairs to the Accounts Department.

"This is Mr. Angus," he said, on arriving at the department. "He'll be in charge of the machine, if we have it."

"Glad to meet you," said Brown. "And I'm sure you'll be pleased that I've called when you get this machine installed. I know you won't mind my saying so, but—you're a Scotsman and won't like to see money thrown about. Well, this machine's going to save the firm pounds. You'll appreciate that because, if the firm doesn't waste money, there's more for all of you— that's right, isn't it?"

"Aye," said Angus. "Maybe!"

They walked towards the filing system, where thousands of accounts were filed, and a young boy was busily inserting cards. Brown didn't take any notice of him, but got to work straight away on the estimate for the machine required.

Into the office walked a blonde—and a well-made blonde at that. "What's going on here?" she asked.

Harrison explained to her what Brown was doing, and it

was evident from the conversation that the blonde was Mr. Davies' secretary. She started up a conversation with Brown, and they were soon busily chatting about this and that.

"Are you the representative for this area, then?" said the blonde.

"Not exactly," said Brown. "Actually I'm the assistant sales manager. I do come on special jobs like this, though."

It seemed to impress the blonde—at least Brown thought it did. But when she left him he thought he heard her saying to another member of the staff as she passed out of the room, "Another assistant sales manager! There are a few of them about, aren't there!"

He felt a little uncomfortable, but at that moment the managing director walked into the accounts department himself.

"How are you getting on?" he said.

"I've got it all worked out," said Brown. "It's really going to do a good job here."

"What do you think of it, Angus?" asked Davies.

"Not much!" said Angus.

That shook Brown badly.

"How much is it going to cost?" asked the managing director.

Brown gave an approximate figure.

"That seems fair enough."

Brown's spirits rose again.

Once more Harrison interjected, "I still think we ought to get another quote."

"Yes," said Davies. "Perhaps you're right, perhaps you're right. Well, I must say this looks the type of thing we need, but we'll get another quotation. Thank you for calling, Mr. Brown, and Mr. Harrison will get into touch with you if we can do any business with you. Goodbye."

"Goodbye," said Brown, and he could almost feel his heart tickling his heels.

That's the end of the story. It *is* only a story and, of course, it has been slightly exaggerated. But I have seen all that I have written happen in practice on various occasions.

How many mistakes in human relationship have you found? Have you found the thirteen? Good! Read on, and check up with yourself.

You haven't? Go back to the beginning and read it all again.

Don't say it couldn't have happened. These things actually do happen and are happening every day.

All I am concerned with is the fact that YOU will never be guilty of letting yourself make these errors.

DID YOU SPOT THESE MISTAKES IN HUMAN RELATIONSHIP?

1. *Always be Courteous*

If Brown had understood the necessity for always being courteous he would have acted as follows:

First, he would have telephoned his sales manager to make certain that he was not calling at an inconvenient time.

Secondly, on arriving at his manager's office he would not have taken off his coat until invited by the sales manager to do so. ARE YOU ALWAYS COURTEOUS?

2. *Be Sympathetic*

Self-pity never did anybody any good, but now and again we all feel the need of sympathy.

Evans, the sales manager, was obviously busy. But that, possibly, didn't worry him so much as the fact that his doctor had just told him that he had a duodenal ulcer.

Brown merely mentioned that he was sorry to interrupt Evans when he was busy, and then went on with the reason for his call. When Evans told him of his ailment Brown should immediately have expressed sympathy, and he might even have cheered his sales manager up by telling him of cases that he, perhaps, knew personally of men who had had suspected ulcers which further investigation had proved to be something quite harmless.

A little sympathy on Brown's part, and the meeting would have got off to a much better start.

3. *Good Manners*

We all know that it is not considered good manners for a salesman to enter a shop, house, or office, while smoking a cigarette or pipe. Only a man who is completely thick-skinned or has no knowledge whatsoever of human relationships would do such a thing.

There is another offence which a cigarette-smoking salesman sometimes makes which is almost as bad as walking into an office smoking. That is when he offers a cigarette which the other person refuses, and then smokes one himself.

It is true that Evans had told the salesman he could smoke, but he could hardly do otherwise.

A salesman can lose a big order through making this mistake.

A busy executive was trying to cut down his smoking, and was limiting himself to six cigarettes a day. In the morning he would have one after his coffee, and then he would not smoke again until after lunch. A salesman, calling to see him after he had finished his after-coffee cigarette, did what Brown did in the story. He offered the managing director a cigarette. The managing director said he didn't want one, but told the salesman to carry on if he wanted to do so. The salesman, having no knowledge of human relations, did just that. This really annoyed the managing director, because as soon as the salesman started to smoke he felt the need to smoke again himself. He didn't want to break his rule and, of course, it would have been rude to light up a cigarette immediately after refusing the salesman's offer.

He didn't let the salesman stay long.

IF THE BUYER WON'T SMOKE WITH YOU, DON'T SMOKE AT ALL.

4. *Criticism*

Many people believe that they are popular because of their bluntness. This isn't so. They may be popular because they are good fellows, good friends, good sportsmen. But not because they are blunt. Bluntness can often be an excuse for rudeness.

Brown made the cardinal error in human relations when he began his protestations to his sales manager. Nobody likes criticism. Remind yourself of that every morning when you wake up, every night when you go to sleep. Nobody likes criticism. Nobody wants your criticism. Even when somebody asks for it they still don't want it.

Obviously, however, on occasion it is essential to criticise, and this is in order—provided you criticise the right way.

It was wrong of Brown to start complaining of his territory, and to talk about bad mistakes, without giving his sales manager the opportunity of saving his face if a mistake had been made. It would have been far wiser for him to have said, "You know you are a very efficient lot here, not much goes wrong, and I can only think that there must have been some typist's error in making out my territory, because I seem to be overlapping."

Words to that effect would have toned down the criticism. The old advice to count ten before losing your temper is just as sound in regard to criticism. Before you open your mouth to criticise anybody, count ten and then, if possible, keep quiet.

5. *Apologise*

Evans was soon able to prove that the mistake in the letter addressed to Brown's customer had been due to Brown's illegible handwriting. As soon as this was pointed out, Brown should have said quickly, "I'm sorry."

It's very difficult indeed to get angry with anyone who says those two words. But sometimes it needs a lot of moral courage to say them.

6. *Keep Your Temper*

Do men who lose their tempers always get their way? Well, if a man is head of an organisation I suppose he can lose his temper as much as he likes and, provided he's thick-skinned and his conscience doesn't prick him when he realises how much he has hurt others, he will be able to go on losing his temper to enable him to win every argument.

The average person, however, gains nothing by this temper-losing business. A salesman must be able to control his own feelings if he wants to succeed.

Let the little men of the world lose their tempers—some of the biggest business magnates are really only little men at heart. Let them all go on shouting and ranting. But you make up your mind to be really big and learn to keep your temper.

7. Admit Your Mistakes

Here, the sales manager was at fault. The territory he had given to Brown was wrongly defined. He tried to excuse the fault and put the blame on Brown's shoulders. He shouldn't have done this. He should have admitted his mistake right away.

That is another point which you must remember. If you do make a mistake—admit it, and admit it quickly and sincerely.

8. Don't Gossip

Brown met his friend Robinson, and they had coffee together. Soon they were talking about another salesman. They were making remarks about the trouble he had had with a girl.

This is the kind of gossip which doesn't do anybody any good. But most of all it does harm to those who actually do the gossiping. Don't agree with a gossiper because you want to be friendly. Keep quiet, and let him talk.

9. Thank You

Those two words can mean so much. A 'thank you' to the man who gives you your newspaper; a 'thank you' to the girl at the telephone exchange who gives you your number; a 'thank you' to the shop assistant; a 'thank you' to the taxi driver, will do the world of good, and can cheer up the recipient for the rest of the day.

Brown, when he was on the bus, ignored the first appeal for fares. Then he asked for a threepenny ticket, but he didn't say 'please'. Neither did he say 'thank you' when the ticket was handed to him. And what happened in consequence? The bus conductor didn't bother to advise him when he came to his stop, so that the omission of that little 'thank you' cost him a half-mile walk.

Remember, politeness is an essential feature of a salesman's make-up.

10. *Make the Other Man Feel Important*

We all suffer because we feel that others do not realise that we are as important as we, ourselves, feel that we are. This is not confined solely to the group of low wage earners. I have seen executives go to endless trouble to try to prove their importance. If you once shatter a man's ideas in this direction you may have lost a friend for ever. Build a man up and you have made a friend.

When the managing director asked Brown about his proposition he said, "I've been explaining it to your clerk." It turned out that Harrison was in charge of the department and was, therefore, either a senior clerk or, perhaps, a junior manager. Anyway, it wouldn't have hurt Brown to have referred to him as 'your manager'. Instead, his reference to 'your clerk' annoyed Harrison, who advised his managing director not to buy until he had obtained other quotations.

ALWAYS MAKE THE OTHER PERSON FEEL IMPORTANT.

11. *Be Tactful*

Fifty per cent of salesmen are most tactless. That is surprising, because you would think that salesmen would be the one group of men who would be most tactful. But this is not so.

Brown made a most tactless remark to Mr. Angus, who right away decided against the machine. But whether it costs you business or not, tactlessness can hurt other people and, when you hurt enough people, you'll lose a lot of friends. And when you have lost enough friends, you will find that life becomes more difficult and depressing. Be tactful at all times. At the end of every day, just run over the day's work to see that you haven't said anything out of place.

12. *Don't Boast*

Nobody likes a man who boasts. So many salesmen seem to wish to hide the fact that they are salesmen. I have known men pretend that they are directors, managers, local managers, assistant sales managers or what you will.

There is no need for that. Not only in your business, but in your private life, avoid all forms of boasting. Needless to say, boasting and lying are very much akin, so also avoid lying. The liar invariably makes mistakes and is generally found out.

Do you like others to boast to you? You don't! Well, then, of course, you will never boast to anyone else, whether what you have to boast about is true or untrue.

13. *Treat All Members of the Staff Alike*

When Brown entered the Accounts Department there was a young man filing some cards. Brown ignored him and went on with his business.

He should have greeted the young man pleasantly, perhaps had a few words with him and built up his feeling of importance, because that was the right and proper thing to do.

A managing director once said to a salesman, "You can afford to be rude to me. I don't mind and, anyway, I can answer you back and stand up for myself. But you can't afford to be rude to my junior staff."

STUDY THIS LESSON

This lesson on Human Relationships can only help you, as I have stressed before, if you are willing, every day of your life, to ask yourself if you have committed any of the errors that you have just been reading about.

Some little while ago I gave a lecture, and during it I mentioned the point about smoking cigarettes in other people's offices. When the lecture was over, one of the salesmen asked to have a few words with me in private. I invited him into my office.

He took out his cigarette case and offered me one. I refused, but told him he could smoke—and he lit up right away.

Only fifteen minutes before he had heard me lecturing on that very subject. If a man can forget a point like this within fifteen minutes of hearing it, then how much more quickly will he forget it if he only reads about it.

This one chapter can help you to succeed. It can help you to earn extra money. It can help you to achieve a high position. . . . But only if you are willing to apply its lessons daily.

Well, are you?

THE GREATEST LESSON IN SELLING

Now here is probably the greatest lesson in salesmanship, and it's one which needs no elaboration.

The two most important words in SALESMANSHIP are:

YOU and WE

There you have the lesson. It needs little explanation. Use the word YOU whenever you possibly can. If that doesn't apply, then bring the prospect along with you, and use the word WE. And only finally bring yourself into the picture.

Remember, YOU—WE—I.

LORD CHESTERFIELD'S TEN POINTS ON HUMAN RELATIONS

Many teachers of human relations and the art of influencing other people have written at great length on this subject, but Lord Chesterfield summed the whole thing up very well many, many years ago when he wrote:

Talk often, but never long. Adapt your conversation to the people with whom you are conversing.   Tell stories seldom, and absolutely never but where they are very apt and very short. Never hold anybody by the button or the hand, in order to be heard out. Avoid in mixed companies argumentative conversation. Avoid speaking of yourself. Always look people in the face when you talk to them. Mimicry, neither practise yourself not applaud in others. Swearing is as silly and as illiberal as it is wicked. Have a frank, open and ingenious exterior with a prudent and reserved interior.

Now study that again and again, and keep on studying it. Lord Chesterfield's advice to his son is also good advice to salesmen.

THE BODY OF WILLIAM JAY

Have you heard this jingle?

> *Here lies the body of William Jay*
> *Who died defending his right of way*
> *He was sure he was right, as he sped along*
> *But he's just as dead as if he were wrong.*

There are so many William Jays about, and there's very little that anybody can do with them. I doubt whether you are a William Jay because, if you were, you wouldn't be reading this book, or you certainly wouldn't be reading it carefully. William Jay would pick it up, glance through a few pages, probably say, "You can't learn salesmanship from a book", and then cast the book aside.

Here are the sort of expressions that William uses:

"My wireless set is the best of its kind. That one that you have is of no use at all."

Or, "There's only one car on the market, that's the one I've got. It's a wonderful job!"

Or, "I always go to Kingston-on-Sea every year. It's the only seaside place worth going to. Wouldn't dream of going anywhere else."

William Jay has a closed mind. He isn't prepared to listen to reason. Once having made up his mind on any subject he won't budge.

It isn't any use always sitting on a fence. A man has to make up his own mind and stand by his decisions. But the thinking man should always be ready to be influenced by the ideas of others if he considers those ideas sound, and if they prove that his decisions may not have been correct.

Open-mindedness is very difficult to achieve and, as people whose minds are closed believe that they are right all the time, they will continue to make mistakes, and then wonder why they don't succeed.

Open-mindedness does not mean weakness. The man who is open-minded usually has great strength of character. It doesn't matter how right you may feel you are in your judgment, always be prepared to listen to the other man. Don't shout him down, don't interrupt him by using such expressions as "Nonsense!" or "Absurd!" Hear him out. When he has had his say, then you're entitled to form your own opinion.

Open-mindedness is a wonderful asset to any salesman.

GESTURES

Lloyd George was a most dynamic speaker, and if he didn't happen to throw both his legs in the air at the same time it was only because he didn't want to fall flat on his face. But his gestures were quite in keeping with his whole make-up. It didn't look incongruous when he waved his hands. The waving was part of his make-up, fitting in well with the way he spoke and acted. If the average salesman tried to do it, however, he would just look silly.

Many a salesman adopts gestures which don't suit him. Too many thump their hands on tables, wave their arms in the air when they get excited, and point too dramatically at their samples. Gestures are useful when selling, but they should be normal actions. They shouldn't be exaggerated and, when required, should be so natural that it would be unnatural not to use them.

Here is an example:

If I were to ask you to describe a spiral staircase, what would you do?

Well, do it. You'd start to talk and then, quite naturally, your hand would go round and round in upward spirals. Do you see what I mean?

WHAT A CAT!

Two women are talking over a garden fence, or chatting away while in a queue. Two men pass by. They smile in a superior manner and one will say to the other, "They're at it again! Someone's losing a reputation, I'll be bound. Why are women so catty?"

Yes, that happens often. But, quite frankly, the whole thing could be reversed, and the women, with all justification, on seeing two or three men together, could say, "Whose name are they taking away?"

You can check this very easily for yourself. Join any group of men and you will find that you are not with them more than half an hour before somebody is being criticised.

That's true enough, isn't it? Well, do you join in? If you do—stop it.

There is a way in which you can become head and shoulders above your fellow men: stop running others down.

And here is a peculiar thing: if you stand up for people; if, whenever you hear somebody being decried, you say, "I haven't found him like that", your friends won't think you are soft, or weak-minded, or anything like that. Gradually, they will form the opinion that you are a very good fellow. When you're not with them, they will say of you, "Yes, he's a good chap. I've never heard him speak ill of anyone."

Possibly you've said that about other people. Make certain in future that they always say it about you.

DON'T BE A SNOB

Here are some quick-changing scenes which are familiar to every salesman.

First, a buying room. Salesmen are grouped together yarning. Standing aside is a salesman who will have nothing to do with the men in the group. He walks about, impatient at the fact that he is being kept waiting, and if he happens to be addressed by anybody entering the buying room, he nods curtly and then looks the other way.

The next scene—a queue of salesmen waiting to see a buyer. They are standing in line until the buyer appears. A little way away from them is a salesman trying to give the impression that he is not really selling anything, that he's probably the managing director of his firm on a goodwill visit.

The next scene is a shop in a busy street. A salesman is conducting his business with a shop owner. A car pulls up, the driver leaves the wheel, slams the car door behind him, hurries into the shop, sees another salesman, but doesn't retreat. He says, "Sorry, Mr. Jones, didn't know you were busy." Mr. Jones then replies, "I shan't be long if you'd like to wait." He then goes over to the newcomer and has a few minutes' chat with him, much to the discomfort of the other salesman who was, possibly, about to get an order.

These scenes will show you the salesman snob at work. This type of man often represents a first-class house, and he feels that, because of this, he should have some form of priority treatment. Sometimes he is the director of his own company, or the son of one of the directors. He wants to do his best to show all the other gentlemen on the road that he is a cut above them.

Salesmen can be of great help to one another. They can give tips about customers, ideas about territories. . . . It's a good thing to be one of them, and if you are a salesman you *are* one of them, so why try to be different?

A MUST FOR EVERY SALESMAN

I was once talking to that great comedian Sid Fields, whose death was such a sad loss to the stage. I was somewhat surprised at the fact that he was rather glum, in fact almost morose, during the conversation which took place. Then suddenly something was said which caused him to smile. Immediately, his whole face lit up, and I thought what a loveable, likeable man he was.

His smile did that. A friendly smile can do more to influence somebody else to be kindly disposed towards you, and to like you, than possibly anything else.

Psychologists now tell us that it isn't strictly correct to say that our mental attitude towards life always affects our physical condition. More often than not our physical condition affects our mind. If we droop our lips it reacts on the mind, and we feel fed up. If we alter our expression and smile, then we begin to feel more cheery. That is something which we can prove for ourselves, and it does work nearly every time.

Turn up the sides of your lips. You'll find it very difficult to feel miserable. Not only then does a smile affect the other person, but it affects just as much the person who is smiling.

Smile in a friendly manner whenever you make an approach, whether it's to an old customer or a new prospect. I heard someone on the radio singing a song recently, and one of the lines was: *Let your heart wear a grin.* Corny? Maybe! But that's the way you should smile—from your heart—just because you think it's good to be alive, it's good to have a good selling job, it's good to meet people.

I once asked a salesman how he had become successful, and he answered: "I smiled my way to success!"

Maybe not strictly true, but wonderful advice.

DON'T BE A FUNNY MAN

A psychiatrist was giving a lecture. Quite a few of us sat upright when he said, "One of the signs of an inferiority complex is when a man must continually tell funny stories." He went on to explain that often a person told these stories to attract attention to himself. Then he said, "Those who suffer more in this respect than others are the people who try to outdo others. Somebody tells a story. The listener is hardly conscious of the story because he is so busy trying to remember one he can tell as soon as his friend has finished talking. That person who continually has to tell bigger and better stories is trying to impress others with his importance."

That is the psychiatrist's theory but, in spite of that, we do like to hear stories on occasion. Not many stories, however, are worth listening to. Some seem to go on and on and never end. Others are punctuated with 'Stop me if you've heard this one'. And then there is the story which is told with loud guffaws on the part of the teller, who can't even wait to finish, to laugh at his own joke.

The strange thing is that we all think we can tell a good story.

Let those who enjoy telling their stories go on telling them to their friends, but here is some advice to you as a salesman: Don't overdo the telling of funny stories.

Some salesmen think they have built up a good name for themselves when others say, perhaps, "Ah, here's Bill. He'll have one for us!"

They have built up a name for themselves—a name of the wrong kind. If ever you have a good story to tell—tell it. And then stop. Don't go on and on and on. There are certain men who can tell one good story and everybody laughs. This encourages them, and they tell another, and another, and another. . . . They try to monopolise the whole party. They do it to buyers too, when selling, but it only bores the buyers.

There's a great deal in what the psychiatrist says.

Cut down on your funny stories, and maybe you'll increase your sales.

NINE WAYS TO MAKE PEOPLE LIKE YOU

Check up on the following points, and check on them regularly. Put a tick against those which line up with your qualities. When you can put a tick against all nine, you'll be on your way to selling yourself to success.

Here they are:

1. Are you always cheerful ?
2. Are you always tolerant?
3. Are you always truthful?
4. Are you honest?
5. Are you dependable?
6. Are you unselfish?
7. Are you modest?
8. Are you grateful?
9. Are you loyal?

Be fair to yourself and check up now. If you can't put a tick against many of these points, see what you can do to put matters right.

TEN IDEAS TO HELP YOU SELL YOURSELF

1. Appreciate other people's interests. You probably know the story of the fond mother watching a platoon of soldiers marching past, which included her son. The mother was heard to express her amazement at the fact that all the platoon were out of step except her Willie.

   Too many people are like that mother. They believe that if they don't get along too well with other people it is always the fault of the other people. To get people to like you you must first show interest in them, their ideas, their hobbies, their businesses.

2. A most important business executive said the other day that he is actually a little lazy. In view of his dynamic energy, that sounded strange coming from him, but it was true enough.

   We are all a little lazy as far as certain jobs are concerned. It always helps a man to sell himself to others if he saves them extra work, so if you can save any of your prospects, customers or friends from additional work—do so.

3. Phillip was very keen on the girl. He was working up enough courage to propose. He decided to take her to the ballet because he knew that she liked ballet. He loathed it, but when he made the suggestion that evening the young lady said, "I didn't know you liked ballet. Do you?" And Phillip answered, "I just love it."

Let's get to the end of the story quickly. They're married now. They never go to ballet any more.

You see, they both loathed it really. She said she liked it because she thought he liked it; and he did, because he thought it was something she admired. In other words, they were both pretending.

To sell yourself to others, don't pretend. Don't pretend you like opera if you don't like it. Don't pretend you're an outdoor man when you'd rather play patience indoors. Be yourself.

4. Will Rogers once said, "I never met a man I did not like." Obviously, he met various kinds of people, good, bad, and indifferent. But he wasn't really interested in their past or in what they were doing. He looked for the good qualities in them, and nearly everyone has certain good qualities.

Here, then, is another tip for selling yourself: always look for the good qualities in others, and you will find something to like about each one of them.

5. Every now and again someone writes a letter to a newspaper complaining at the fact that during a rush hour men have the seats, and old people are left standing, and nothing is done about it.

It is said that manners of people to-day are worse than ever they were, but I am not qualified to judge that.

My advice to you is to cultivate good manners at all times. In your own home, in public, wherever you are—be well mannered. And always remember to be just as well mannered to the assistant as you are to the managing director.

6. In an argument of any kind, *you* have the last word but one. Let the other man get in the last word. Let him go away happy. You go away content that you haven't made an enemy.

7. When selling, a salesman often makes statements or promises that he can't keep. Here is a rule: Never say anything, never make a promise, unless you could put the words down in writing, add your signature, and have it witnessed. If you can't do this, then don't make the promise. People will like you for your integrity.

8. Have you ever tried to bluff your way through something? Sometimes it works, but you're never very happy afterwards. There are three words that can help you a great deal and can make an impression with a prospect. Here they are:

I DON'T KNOW.

Far better to admit honestly that you don't know something than to try to bluff it out.

9. At some time or another we have all said, "That fellow's a know-all!" You've said it, haven't you? Nobody likes a know-all.

Be quite certain that nobody ever says that about you!

10. Too often we hear the expression these days, "It's No. 1 that counts!" Unfortunately, when we think in terms of 'No. 1' we are often the losers.

To get other people to like us and to do things for us, we must first of all see what we can do for the other person.

Read these points again. TO SELL SUCCESSFULLY, A SALESMAN MUST FIRST SELL HIMSELF.

DON'T PULL FACES

Sometimes, when selling, a salesman will call upon a prospect or buyer who turns out to be of foreign extraction—possibly with a slight accent. When this happens, many salesmen alter their style of selling completely. They seem to have the idea that because a man wasn't born in Great Britain he needs to have everything explained to him with a lot of gestures and contortions of the face. I have seen salesmen, when selling to a foreign buyer, speaking very, very slowly, articulating each word, while looking at the buyer as if he were a little simple.

This, of course, is salesmanship at its worst, and it also shows a complete lack of understanding of human relations and good manners. Whoever you sell to, wherever he may come from, whatever his nationality, you should sell to him in exactly the same way as you sell to anyone else.

THREE CERTAIN WAYS OF ACHIEVING POPULARITY

If you don't like the word 'popular'—if you feel that men need not necessarily be popular to get on, then let's substitute another word for it. Would 'likeable' suit you? No, you don't like that either? Then we'll think again.

You know, 'popular' isn't so bad. It means that when a man is popular, people appreciate him, like him to be with them, and will do things for him.

If you are well liked you will influence others, because they will want to be influenced by you. Now this is all you have to do to achieve success in the field of human relations:

1. Always be sincere.
2. Give praise where praise is due.
3. Always give honest appreciation.

Do these three points seem easy to you? You'd think so, wouldn't you?

They're so hard that not one person in two hundred and fifty can ever carry them out satisfactorily.

1. *Sincerity*

Unless you believe in what you are doing you cannot be sincere. You must have absolute faith in what you are selling.

If you haven't this faith then change your job, because without sincerity you cannot succeed.

2. *Give Praise Where Praise is Due*

We all feel better for a little praise, yet we rarely receive it. Do you like to be praised when you do things properly? You do? But do you give praise when others carry out their tasks satisfactorily for you? I have stressed this point for many years at lectures to sales executives as well as salesmen. Everyone agrees with me, and yet afterwards those very same men carry on as they did before, rarely praising anyone.

You make a resolution right now to give praise when it is due every time, and a new life will open up for you. You will make friends more readily, others will want to help you and do things for you.

But don't save your praise for to-morrow. Don't decide to give it this time next week. Do it as the occasion arises.

Praise the shop assistant when she tries to help you. Praise your wife when she has obviously cooked something special for you. Praise the secretary for her help and advice.

As Charles Schwab, head of Bethlehem Steel, once said, "Give praise lavishly."

3. *Always Give Honest Appreciation*

Listen to these remarks—the first by the sales director of one of our largest food combines:

"I sometimes think I have wasted the last ten years. Only a year ago I reorganised the whole of our sales department. We achieved greater success, but I've never had a word of appreciation from the managing director or chairman for what I've done."

And again, the manager of a bookshop—a branch of an organisation controlling many shops:

"I've worked this week from seven in the morning until midnight because the shop is being altered, and I wanted to make a space for the builders so that we shouldn't lose any trade next day. I feel exhausted. I wouldn't have minded if I had had just a letter of appreciation, or a 'phone call telling me that they appreciated what I was doing."

And thirdly, a gardener:

"I nearly broke my back to pick up that lot. I got it done in time, luckily, because the weather changed. But you know money isn't everything. I've been paid a bit extra for it, but if only she'd given me a few words of appreciation. After all, I needn't have done it."

Every one of those statements tells its own story. Men in all walks of life have felt the need for appreciation that wasn't given. But here's something you should ask for yourself now:

Did the sales manager of the food company show appreciation towards the others working for him? Did the bookshop manager appreciate his staff or his customers? Did the gardener show any appreciation for the work which may have been done on his behalf?

We're back to the same thing—we all need appreciation, and when we get it we feel much better for it. Make up your mind right now that whenever anyone does anything for you, you will show your appreciation for what has been done.

FIVE MISTAKES TO AVOID

Miss Carmody is a buyer for a London store, and she probably sees as many salesmen each day as any buyer anywhere. This is the advice she gives to a young salesman making his first approach:

"When you walk towards me, don't slouch. It gives me the impression that you haven't any confidence in what you are selling. But don't show off, either.

"If I send my assistant over to tell you I'm ready to see you, walk straight towards me. Don't hesitate as if I were an ogre. You need not be nervous if you have faith in your products.

"When you arrive, don't shake hands unless I offer to shake hands with you. I always do shake hands with my friends in the trade, but I don't want to shake hands with everyone—especially the man who arrives blowing his nose.

"Finally, if you do shake hands with me, don't try to be the strong man and break my bones."

That's good advice from Miss Carmody. Learn from it. The correct way to act is to walk briskly towards a buyer in a confident manner, and not to offer to shake hands unless the buyer extends his or her hand first.

DON'T BE SCARED OF BEING SCARED

During a broadcast, a man who had been awarded a Victoria Cross was asked by the interviewer, "How did you feel?" He was referring to the feelings of the soldier while the action took place.

The answer was very short. "Scared stiff!"

The hearts of millions of listeners must have warmed at hearing that remark. Here was a man who had shown tremendous courage, saying that he had felt afraid.

Many people feel scared at meeting others. The majority hide it—some successfully, some unsuccessfully. Others try to overcome it by being brazen, curt, or overbearing.

Here is a good point to remember—if ever you are a little worried about feeling afraid, *tell the other man.*

A young man came to see me for a job a little while ago. I sat him down and said, "How are you?"

He answered, "I'm afraid I'm a little nervous."

I chuckled. He chuckled. I did my best to help him, and I am quite certain that within a few seconds he wasn't feeling nervous any longer.

FOUR WAYS TO IMPROVE YOUR VOICE

1. Make up your mind not to gabble.
2. Vary the pitch of your voice occasionally. It is always as well to lower the voice slightly when ending a sentence or making a definite point.

3. Use simple words. Long unwieldy words don't cut any ice. A well-known author once gave this advice on writing: *Make it simple. Whenever you have written a long word, try to think of a simple one, and then substitute it.* That's good advice for a speaker as well.

4. Use emphasis correctly. For example, a man might arrive home late in the evening and find a really wonderful meal cooked ready for him by his wife. He might say, "WHAT a woman!" The emphasis on the 'what' would convey to his wife his admiration for her. During the evening his wife might tell him the story of a neighbour who was neglecting her child, and he might say again, "*What* a woman!" but the tone of his voice and the emphasis would be entirely different.

Later, he might be looking through his favourite magazine and see a well-posed photograph of a rather glamorous-looking film star. Again he might say, "What a *woman*!" And once more he would mean something different.

Here, then, you see three examples of a person using the same three words, but varying the emphasis as circumstances require. Now remember that when selling. With a slight alteration to the tone of your voice you can strengthen every selling sentence.

DEVELOP YOUR OWN PERSONALITY

I know one managing director who employs a good many executives, and if you are with any one of them and you close your eyes you can imagine that you are talking to the managing director himself. If you then open your eyes and take little notice of their features, you will see that all their gestures are the same as those used by their chief.

Every man should try to improve his personality, but the best way to do that is to develop your own personality. It isn't any use trying to copy someone else. Actors can probably do this, but we are not all actors.

Far better check up on yourself to see in which way you can develop your own personality. If your smile is a half-hearted affair—well, turn it into a nicer smile. But make it *your* smile —no one else's. If at some time you've heard a charming man making flattering remarks and getting away with it—don't try to copy him. But if you rarely make kind remarks or praise people for the good things they do, well, then, in your own way, alter your personality and try giving this praise.

"Be yourself" is good advice to a salesman, provided he is never really satisfied with himself, but continually tries to improve his own personality.

CHAPTER IX

The Right Way to Handle Objections

Salesmen should always welcome objections which signify that a prospect or customer is really only seeking further information. Sometimes objections are used automatically. The buyer is then only attempting to show his authority, his knowledge, or his shrewdness.

THREE MAGIC WORDS

When Mike arrived to join us for coffee we scorched our tonsils and plugged our mouths with bath buns so as to get out quickly. Sometimes he turned up while we were queueing to see a buyer. Then there was no retreat.

Mike was an argumentative character. Nothing wrong in that, but he lost his temper so quickly when anyone disagreed with him. He could never give credit to points made by others—he would brush them aside.

Too many people think that the way to win an argument is to show strength by wading in forcefully from the gong. Many a salesman thinks that the enthusiastic thing to do is not to wait for the prospect to complete his objection, but to start answering it quickly.

THAT IS ALL WRONG

The correct technique is to use the 'three-word' formula. First, listen carefully to what the other person has to say. Nod sagely now and again to give him the impression that you think he is right. That makes him relax. Then, just as he thinks he has won a victory, you quietly say your three magic words:

"I AGREE, BUT——"

When you say *I agree*, the prospect relaxes even more, and

feels that he has won a victory. When you then add *but*, you strengthen your argument to follow.

When answering an objection, then, always remember the three magic words, "I AGREE, BUT——"

YOU AND THE LION TAMER

It was P. Brown, director of the National Cash Register Company, who said to me, "We don't stress objections at our sales training course. We believe it better for the salesmen to be able to forestall the objection by using a better sales story."

This came back to my mind when a sales executive invited me to a conference. The executive put over an excellent objection session, his answers really were scintillating. Afterwards I said to him, "You know, if the prospect doesn't happen to raise some of the objections you have been talking about, your salesmen are going to let him down."

"Why?" he asked.

"Because," I answered, "the prospect won't hear some of the most brilliant parts of your sales story."

All this brings me to the lion tamer.

A famous lion tamer once, on being asked what was the secret of his success, said, "A lion tamer must always be one move ahead of the lion, because if the time ever comes when the lion is one move ahead, that will be the end of his days as a lion tamer."

This applies very strongly to the salesman. So long as he is ahead of the prospect he is doing well. But the minute the prospect is ahead of him he is on the way to losing the order. When a prospect raises a strong objection it often shows that he is ahead of the salesman.

It is quite true that a salesman should welcome objections, but he should not welcome too many of them. It is far better to have one or two objections to deal with than a dozen. The way to head off a prospect is to think of every conceivable answer to every objection he could raise to buying, and then see how many of these answers you can incorporate in your sales talk.

FOUR WAYS TO IMPROVE YOUR ANSWERING OF OBJECTIONS

1. Some salesmen seem to take an objection as a personal affront and, because of that, snap back their answers before the prospect has completed his query. This is something that doesn't happen just once or twice, but on hundreds of occasions. It is usually caused by the salesman having the perfect answer to an objection, and feeling that the prospect is a little ridiculous even to raise it. He therefore snaps back his reply.

   That is quite wrong! You should pause before you answer an objection and, when you answer it, do so in a businesslike manner. *Never be snappy—it doesn't pay!*

2. One of the finest ways of answering any objection is to use it as a sales point. The way to do that is to turn the objection round so that it appears that the prospect is giving you a reason for BUYING instead of one for not buying.

   There is hardly an objection raised to which the answer cannot be prefaced by, "But that is the very reason why you should have this. . . ." Even the most difficult of all objections, "My shelves are full", can sometimes be answered by using this sentence.

   Think of all the objections you have to answer in your day's selling, and see how you can use the above answer with every one of them.

3. Sales Manager E. Lewis told me that he always agrees that a salesman should smile, because that denotes the fact that the salesman is pleased at making a new contact or renewing an old one. But he says that the time when a salesman should look most pleased is when he is faced with an objection.

   By this Mr. Lewis means that a salesman should always be pleased to answer an objection, because this proves to the prospect that the salesman is doing everything possible to help him clear up his queries.

4. J. S. Skinner, Sales Controller of Remington Rand, told me that he believes too many salesmen try to argue on too many fronts at the same time. By this he means that the salesman may be faced with five objections to buying his products. Mr. Skinner thinks there is only one real objection, and the other four don't matter very much. He says, therefore, that a salesman must find, during the sale, the main objection. He should isolate that objection, and towards the end of the sale he can use it as a sales point by saying, "I believe your main reason for not placing an order is . . ." When he gets the prospect's agreement on that, he knows that he has isolated the main objection, *and if he deals with it satisfactorily he will get the order.*

THREE RULES FOR ANSWERING INSULTING OBJECTIONS

1. Don't be too eager to answer this kind of objection quickly. Take your time.
2. When a customer's objection is caused by a grievance, do not interrupt him. Wait until he has got everything off his chest, and before giving your views apologise for what has occurred, use the magic word 'but', and then give your viewpoint.
3. If a prospect makes a highly critical remark about your goods or your company, pretend you have not understood him properly, and ask him to repeat his insulting remarks. Very rarely will he re-state his criticism with the same harshness. This makes the objection easier for you to handle.

MY SHELVES ARE FULL

This is the most difficult objection of all to overcome. It continually faces the seller of staple goods. Sometimes, of course, it is an excuse to get rid of a salesman, and he should always make quite certain before he leaves the shop that he is being told the truth.

The standard answers to this objection are, "That is the reason why you should place an order. It will help you to clear the other goods off your shelves"; or, "This is a quick-selling line. It will bring customers into your shop and, because of that, will give you the opportunity to sell them some of the other goods on your shelves."

These answers can be used, but when your customer tells you that his shelves are full of *your* goods and, for this reason, he cannot buy any more from you for the time being there is little that you can do about it.

The mistake is one of policy. When you first sold the customer those goods you, or your firm, should have done something about helping him to sell them. Did you have the right kind of showcard? Did you advise him on display? Did you make sure that the goods were shown on the counter? Did you try to tie up any advertising campaign with his sales?

Think about these things. It is so easy to over-sell, and it is very hard to undo the harm that may result. Good merchandising is the only real way to tackle this problem.

As I have mentioned before, it is always right to get as big an order as you can because that will allow goods to be shown properly, but some customers haven't the ability to push a line or to make good displays. Those are the customers you must watch carefully and help when you first take their orders. If you do that you won't be met with the objection, "My shelves are full of your goods." Help your customer, so that he can help you!

THE SAME

Of all the hundreds of questions which crop up at our sales training courses the one we hear most frequently is from salesmen selling staple goods. Here is the kind of question we are asked:

"My product is very similar to that of my competitors; the price is the same, and our delivery is the same. How can I get the customer to buy from me, instead of from the other man?"

We have had this question raised by salesmen selling foodstuffs, chemists' sundries, confectionery, paper, hardware, steel-tubing, ductwork, electric lights, and a host of other goods. There is no answer so far as salesmanship is concerned. No amount of good selling will overcome this problem. Trickery will get you nowhere. Promises which cannot be kept will act as a boomerang and, on subsequent calls, you will be worse off than ever. No, there is only one answer, and that is dealt with in the chapters of this book dealing with human relations.

The answer is this: *All things being equal, the customer will always buy from the salesman he likes the best.*

If you study human relations carefully, then the other salesmen will ask this question, but you will do so less and less.

I'LL THINK IT OVER

Delay excuses are often difficult to overcome. We all use them over and over again. I'm sure you have at times been in a shop wondering whether you should buy something and have said, "I'll think it over." You were undecided. You didn't know whether you wanted to buy or not, and the shop assistant couldn't make you come to a decision. At other times, perhaps, you have said, "I'd like to ask my wife about that", or "I'll certainly have it, but not just at the moment. I'll have to buy it later, when I can afford it."

These, then, are the main delay excuses:

"*I'll think it over.*"

"*I want to consult my partner (wife, husband, manager, etc.).*"

"*I'll buy later, when I can afford it.*"

There are, of course, stock answers to these objections, such as:

"What is there to think over? I have explained everything clearly to you. What point haven't I made quite clear?"

"I appreciate that you want to consult your partner, but is that fair to him? He won't have the whole proposition put to him as I have put it to you. Because of this, he may veto the whole thing, which will mean a loss to both of you. . . ."

"I quite understand that you want to buy later when you can afford it. But by buying now you will have so many benefits that, as I have explained to you, the outlay won't be an expense at all—at least, not for long."

These are the stock answers and they can be used occasionally, but they rarely alter the prospect's mind. Whenever a delay excuse is used you know that you have made an imperfect job of selling. If you receive a blank refusal, then possibly the prospect is not in a position to place an order with you. When, however, he tries to put you off, then usually he is in a position to buy, but you haven't made up his mind for him.

Remember what happened when you were in that shop and you nearly bought that shirt? You'd have bought it all right if the shop assistant had made a better sale!

The same applies when you are the salesman. If you rarely meet the delay objection, you know you are selling well. If you meet it often, then improve your sales technique, and you will hear these objections less and less.

THE PRICE BOGEY

Eighty-four prospects who had been approached to buy a specialised service had used every conceivable type of excuse for not buying, ranging from "I want to consult my partner" to "I am moving to other premises".

They were subsequently questioned in detail regarding their reasons for not placing the order by a director of the company selling the service. He spent some time checking up to try to find the *real* reason for his salesmen not making the sale.

He found that the excuses given and the objections raised were not, in fact, the real reasons for the prospects not buying Eighty-one of them admitted that their true objection to buying was one of price. They did not feel like spending so much money.

I think that a similar analysis of the objections raised against buying many of the goods on the market would show that the excuses "I'm overstocked", or "I'll wait till your next journey", or "I'll buy after alterations have been made", etc., etc., are only excuses, and that the real objection to buying is the question of price. That is always the hidden objection.

Now let me put it as simply as this:

So long as the price looms large in the prospect's mind no salesman will ever succeed in closing the sale. An order can only be obtained when the prospect realises that the benefits he will receive by placing it far outweigh the amount of capital he will have to spend to receive those benefits.

Very few salesmen sell benefits sufficiently. They talk about their products, but not about the advantages to the prospect of placing an order for them.

Remember, then, the main reason for not getting orders is because you have not sold benefits sufficiently.

BE SURE YOUR BENEFITS ALWAYS OUTWEIGH THE PRICE FACTOR

THREE WAYS OF HANDLING THE PRICE OBJECTION

Of all the things which seem to scare salesmen, the price of the goods they are selling seems to frighten them most of all. This doesn't really apply to top-ranking salesmen, but a sales force is composed in the main of average salesmen, and it is these men who boggle when they have to give the price of their product to the prospect.

The strange part about this is that men selling cheap goods have the same fear as those selling expensive articles. If they are selling cheap goods then they are worried that the prospect is going to feel that they are selling an inferior product because of the low price quoted. If they are selling a quality article, then they think they are almost certain to get the 'can't afford it' objection.

Too many salesmen ask for this objection. They do it by

showing their fear. When asked the price they either put over a belligerent act (by that I mean they bark out the amount with a 'so what' expression), or they become rabbits and try to scuttle away when the buyer, apparently, glares at them.

Whenever a salesman has to give the price of his product he should remember the following rules:

1. By having a planned sales sequence he should try to explain as many benefits as he possibly can before he has to give the price.

2. When he gives the price of his product he should proceed with his sales story without pausing. In other words, he should not expect any comment on the part of the prospect. If he waits for one it will always be, "What a lot of money!"—a stock phrase we all use when we buy anything.

3. Sometimes it is a good thing to preface the price with the word 'only', but if you are selling a quality product at a high price then it is absurd to use this word. Your price is justified because of the quality of the goods you are selling, and there is no need to try to minimise it unless you say it this way: "Well, sir, when you consider the value we are offering, the price is low. It is only ..."

Remember, then, DON'T BE SCARED OF THE PRICE. Do all you can to strengthen your sales talk, and less and less will you hear the remark, "That's a lot of money!"

PRIDE OF PRICE

There are two types of salesmen—those who are scared of quality, and those who are frightened of price. If a salesman is selling a cheap, shoddy article he is conscious of this and he sells badly.

Now I sympathise with that salesman because, if a man is only selling on price he can have a tough time indeed. But a salesman selling a good commodity should never be afraid, however high the price may be.

One way of overcoming this nervousness is for the salesman

to be proud of the price he charges. When the price query was raised at a meeting of salesmen selling office equipment, the leading salesman said, "I bring the price up myself in this way: 'You know, sir, we're dearer than every competitor, but look at the value we're offering you'."

That man is proud of his price. You should be the same.

THE 'GRUMBLE' OBJECTION

There is a certain type of customer who never raises one specific objection but grumbles all the way through the sale about your goods, your prices, your service, and everything connected with your company.

When you meet this type of grumbling objector the thing to do, of course, is to answer the objections in a kindly manner, but most of all to let the prospect grumble.

Let him go on until he has got the grumbling out of his system; also give way on a small point, and apologise. If you let him have his grumbles, agree with him on one part, and then kindly, but firmly, explain your whole proposition, you will make your sale.

MAYBE HE DOESN'T LIKE THE ANTARCTIC

Unless you are offering some special bargain line, most buyers have the idea that whatever they are buying costs too much. Because of this they are price conscious.

Look at the word PRICE and, having looked at it, remember a rule—

Take the ICE out of PRICE and you won't see the prospect becoming suddenly frigid when you mention the cost of your product. Do this by warming him up on the quality of your goods before you mention the price.

IN A HURRY

You will never get a sale by gabbling through your sales sequence in a few minutes. Yet many salesmen do this when prospects say to them, "I'm in a hurry. Tell me quickly what it's all about."

The best answer to this 'hurry' objection is to say, "You know, sir, I have much too much respect for you to try to tell you about my products in a few minutes. You are not the type of man who would come to a decision on scanty information, and I should be giving you incomplete information about my goods if I were to try and tell you about them quickly."

HOW INEXPENSIVE!

A salesman selling office furniture—the most expensive of its kind—told me that when showing his catalogue of desks to a prospective buyer he will often say, "Do you know that you can actually buy a mahogany desk of this quality for a hundred and eighty pounds?"

He told me that this question brought about a good reaction, because it indicated to the prospect that although he was buying the best desk of its kind he was getting a bargain.

However highly priced the article that you are selling may be, you must be certain to convey the impression that it is extremely good value.

I CAN'T AFFORD IT

If you are in a position to do so you will, of course, show how Leasing—Hire Purchase—Credit Facilities—Factoring—will enable the prospect to purchase without greatly affecting his net profits or cash flow.

Sometimes even experienced managing directors are not fully aware of tax allowances on capital goods, which could have an effect on the cash needed for the purchase over a period of time.

If none of these suggestions apply you could say something like this to prove to the prospect that he can afford to place an order:

"Mr Brown, this machine will cost you only £1500. If we write it off over three years—and, of course, it will last you for many many years longer than that, it means that it will cost you £500 a year, ignoring tax allowances—that is, £10 a week, or £2 a day. In many businesses similar to your own, that amount is lost each day by waste of heating, lighting, telephone calls and letter writing. Mr. Brown, this may not apply to you, but you will agree that there must be some wastage in this direction, and it is only £2 a day that you have to think about— £2 a day, which will bring in a return for you of . . ."

SHE NEVER LETS ME FINISH WHAT I HAVE TO SAY

Do you know any henpecked husbands? If you do, it's almost certain that at some time or another they would like to make use of the sentence with which I have headed this article. Probably the majority of married men, henpecked or not, at some time or another have the feeling that their wives won't wait to hear the whole of their views before voicing an opinion. Of course, if we were to discuss the matter with the wives then I think they would reverse the story. Hubby never lets them finish a sentence before he dogmatically states his views.

You must always remember that when a customer or prospect is raising an objection to buying he is stating his views. You may not like to hear them, you may strongly disagree with them, you may have the answer to them on the tip of your tongue, but do let him have his say. Let him talk himself out. He will feel much better for telling you all about the problem as he sees it. Also, you must bear in mind that if you interrupt him half way through his objection you may not have heard the whole objection, and you may be answering the weakest part of his reasoning because he may have a stronger point up his sleeve.

LET THE PROSPECT HAVE HIS SAY.

ONE, TWO, BUTTON MY SHOE . . .

Few salesmen have not experienced the retort from a prospect or buyer: "You're the fourth man I've seen to-day with . . ." It happens both to speciality salesmen and men selling staples. For example, if you are selling scales, you may be met with: "You're the fourth man I've had here this morning trying to sell me scales."

The right answer to this is: "Yes, sir, that's only natural. In a shop as up to date as yours obviously any salesman selling scales would know that at some time or another you are going to instal the most modern weighing equipment. That's why every scales salesman will keep calling upon you. I'm here with the best. . . ."

TURN THE PROSPECT'S OBJECTION TO YOUR OWN ADVANTAGE.

OBJECTION: I CAN BUY CHEAPER

This is an objection which the majority of salesmen have to deal with regularly. The standard replies: "Nothing has been manufactured which cannot be made cheaper", and "The man who sells a cheap article knows what's wrong with it", don't always work. If a customer has bought a cheaper article than you are selling and has sold it reasonably well, obviously he won't agree with your answers.

Here is another way in which you can tackle this objection:

"I appreciate that you can buy cheaper, sir, but isn't the answer 'will my products sell more?' By that I mean, it isn't so much a question of what you pay for the goods you buy as it is a question of the quantity you sell. You know Jones & Co., don't you? Well, they used to sell the same ties as you are selling. Then they switched to ours and put up their turn-over by some twenty per cent. Mr. Jones will confirm that to you. Of course, he's an old customer of ours, but the other day I opened a new account with Smith's and they find they are doing very much better with my range than they ever did with any other. If my ties sell more than the present lines you are stocking then, even if you do have to pay a little more for our goods, it's well worth your while to place an order with us."

OBJECTION: I ALWAYS BUY FROM JONES—HE'S BEEN A FRIEND OF MINE FOR TWENTY YEARS

The 'he's a friend of mine' objection is one of the hardest to overcome.

First of all, you should show your appreciation of his loyalty to his friend—"Yes, Mr. Brown, I know Jones and his company very well indeed, and they're a fine firm. They've done a lot for the trade. Jones has been a friend of mine for years. But I want to put it to you this way, sir—knowing how good Jones and his firm are, and also that you have done business with them for twenty years—I would not call to see you unless I had a product that was better value than theirs."

Quite a strong argument.

THE TRIVIAL OBJECTION

Every salesman receives his quota of trivial objections. For example, if you happen to be selling profit-making equipment, the prospect might say to you, "I don't want to make any more profit."

That is an example of a frivolous objection. If you treat it as a real objection you will soon find yourself in an argument, and that must be avoided at all costs. The rule to remember with this type of objection is IGNORE IT, and go on with your sales story.

DON'T REDUCE THE PRICE

The telephone bell rang. Holland, the sales manager, lifted the receiver. "Hello," he said, "oh, hello, Wilkins, how are you? Where are you speaking from? Oh, yes. What is it they want? You know we can't do that. Will I speak to him? Yes, all right, put him on the 'phone. Hello, Mr. Smetham, I'm very glad to hear that you are interested in our brushes. I'd certainly like to have your account. We can, if we reduce the price! All right, Mr. Smetham, but I'll leave it to you. You tell me how we can reduce the price and I'll reduce it. Yes, I know, Mr. Smetham, but just listen to this: we buy our raw material in the best possible market—I'm quite prepared to give you the name of our suppliers if you wish. They won't reduce their prices and we wouldn't ask them to do so. If they

did they'd only reduce the quality, and that wouldn't be any
good to us or to our customers. We can't, then, reduce the
price of the raw material. Labour? You know you can't play
about with labour charges. They have fixed rates. If we reduced
those rates there'd be a strike. We couldn't do that, could
we? Overheads? Yes, that's the standard answer, reduce the
overheads. But I should explain that we have recently had a
firm of efficiency experts in who absolutely tooth-combed our
whole building—office and works—to reduce our overheads.
They could find little to reduce, and we certainly can't get it
down any more so we're left with profit. Well, sir, if we reduced
our profits there wouldn't be any sense in trading, would
there? You wouldn't want to trade at a loss, would you? You
see then, sir, that it isn't easy to find any way to reduce prices.
What's that? You'll place your order? Thank you very much,
Mr. Smetham, I thought you would. Goodbye."

Ask the prospect how you can reduce your prices, and sometimes he will pay the price you ask.

SIX POINTS TO REMEMBER WHEN ANSWERING OBJECTIONS

1. You must quash the objection completely. If you feel
   that you haven't satisfactorily dealt with it, then keep
   on until you have entirely eradicated it from the
   prospect's mind.
2. As soon as you feel that you have dealt satisfactorily
   with an objection, don't bring it up again. Don't go on
   talking about it. Get right on with your sales talk.
3. If you cannot answer an objection efficiently, don't get
   into an argument with the prospect. Rather give way
   on the point, and start selling him from a different angle.
4. Try to avoid bringing up any controversial points
   yourself which may put an objection into the prospect's
   mind.
5. Always try to develop an objection to your own advantage by turning it into a sales point.

6. When a prospect raises an objection it is often a good thing to find out if it is the main objection by saying: "And have you any other reason for not buying, sir?"

I DON'T NEED IT

When answering this type of objection it is sometimes useful to remember that the prospect need not necessarily be a selfish person. You can often best tackle this objection by answering, "Well, sir, change the 'I' to 'We' and then see if you can give me the same answer."

He may look a little amazed, but then you can add, "You said that you didn't need it, sir. But could you say, 'We don't need it'?" The 'we', of course, referring perhaps to his wife or members of his staff.

This answer is often used by insurance salesmen, or salesmen selling equipment for the welfare of the staff.

RAISE THE MAIN OBJECTION

Sometimes a salesman is so scared of an objection which he knows will be raised that he sells badly because of that fear. As soon as he feels that the prospect is about to raise the objection he hedges him off and talks about something else.

This is bad selling. If there is a main objection, it is sometimes a good plan to bring it out yourself and deal with it.

A friend of mine sold confectionery for a small manufacturer. The larger manufacturers, his competitors, advertised extensively. He was always being met with the objection, "My customers ask for advertised sweets." This so scared my friend that there came a time when he hardly liked to make a call.

Finally, he decided to take the bull by the horns and alter his approach. Soon after he made his approach he would say to the prospect, "We don't advertise extensively, but we do something which we think is even better than that. We put the money we would spend on advertising into our sweets. That means that we can give such good value that your customers, once they have bought our confectionery, will come back to your shop for more."

Do you see what he did? He brought out his main objection right away, and then did his best to kill it.

Now, of course, his firm have become one of the larger concerns, and spend a lot of money on advertising, so maybe he won't mind my giving this tip to other confectionery salesmen who represent the smaller firms.

NEVER BE AFRAID TO RAISE THE MAIN OBJECTION YOURSELF.

CHAPTER X

Sales Aids—and How to Use Them

WHEN a salesman demonstrates properly he always holds the interest of the prospect or customer. But a bad demonstration can lose a sale. All salesmen demonstrate—some with pencil and paper, others with leaflets, and some with samples or working models.

It is important that every salesman should master the art of demonstration.

BRINGING THE RABBIT OUT OF THE HAT

The stage magician knows that the quickness of the hand deceives the eye. He also realises that the slowness of the hand makes the eye look more keenly. Maskelyne used to give this advice to would-be conjurors: *Don't rush.* Carl Hertz, another great magician famous for his bird-in-a-cage disappearing act, gave the same advice: *Take your time.*

In view of the fact that when watching a disappearing bird-in-a-cage trick, or seeing a chair suddenly turn into a bowl of flowers, it all happens so quickly that the advice to slow everything down seems rather contrary to what actually happens. But is it? If you took the act of an average conjuror it probably wouldn't contain more than five or six main tricks. How, then, does he fill in his ten or fifteen minutes? By making you want to see those tricks which are all over in a flash. That, in show business, is called showmanship.

In a way, salesmen are in show business. They have to go on working when they feel like giving up. They have to take a lot of failures before they achieve success; and, most of all, *they have to be showmen.* But, and this is the point, we all know that stage acts indulge in showmanship. We must remember, however, that a salesman, although he has to be a perfect showman, *must, at all times, give the exact opposite impression.*

There is one way in which a salesman can improve his showmanship tremendously. He can remember the advice of Maskelyne and Carl Hertz, and *take his time.* By that I mean take his time before showing his sales aids.

It is so easy to pick out the weak salesman. In he walks, bag in hand. Soon it is open, and the desk or counter is littered with leaflets, which cause an unfavourable reaction on the part of the prospect.

The top-grade salesman uses far fewer leaflets, but he *uses them properly.* He produces the leaflet. Then he goes on talking for a few minutes to arouse the interest of the prospect. He is about to open the leaflet when he stops and says a few more words. . . . Most of us are born inquisitive, and every prospect, treated in this manner, is eager to see what is in the leaflet.

From now on use showmanship when showing your sales aids. Before you produce that newspaper cutting, or a testimonial letter, or that diagram which you took so long to work out to prove your point—HESITATE. The slower you are in revealing to the prospect what is written in your literature, THE STRONGER WILL BE ITS APPEAL when you eventually, DRAMATICALLY, make your point with its aid.

SIX WAYS OF DEMONSTRATING

If you use a demonstration model, or you show your samples, remember to explain some of the main selling features of your equipment or articles *before* you demonstrate. And remember these points as well :

1. If your demonstration unit is not in perfect condition, refuse to work with it. Take it back to your company and ask them to change it.

2. Never apologise for a demonstration unit because it is not working correctly, due to some slight defect which may have occurred at a previous call. If this has happened, don't demonstrate at all.

3. Let the prospect sell himself by allowing him to work your model.

4. Demonstrate slowly. Make sure that your prospect is following each point.

5. Make sure that you know everything about your demonstration model, so that if anything should go wrong during the demonstration, you can put it right without the prospect being aware of what has happened.

6. If your demonstration model can, in any way, damage furniture or stain anything, be quite certain before you start to operate it that it can in no way harm the prospect's furniture or furnishings.

HANDLING LITERATURE

The amateur salesman always handles his literature badly, and often the professional doesn't make sufficient use of his sales aids. By literature I mean catalogues, leaflets, or books containing descriptions or specifications of the equipment which is being sold, or showing photographs taken of installations, or reproductions of testimonial letters. In fact, any printed matter which helps the sale along.

The point to remember about sales literature is that prospects, although interested in a picture, will very rarely read pages of printed matter. Salesmen over and over again produce a good sales aid, start to talk about it, and perhaps point to a reproduction of a report. The prospect shows interest and holds out his hand for the leaflet which the salesman hands to him. Then the prospect apparently reads the leaflet through, and the salesman thinks he is making good headway. But the prospect is not reading it at all. He is glancing at it, probably thinking all the while of a way to get rid of the salesman.

Some sales executives believe that a salesman should hand his leaflet over to the prospect and then stand back, so that the prospect can give his undivided attention to what he is reading. I don't agree with that because, in the first place, I don't think the prospect ever does read it line by line and, secondly, if he does, I don't believe he understands it properly.

No prospect wants to read through a page of printed matter. All the salesmen can do is point out to him the main features of interest. It is not, therefore, wise to hand the literature to the prospect. The salesman should retain possession of it and read through the important passages to the prospect, stressing each point in turn.

This, of course, does not apply to a photograph which the prospect may want to examine. But even in the case of the photograph the salesman should point out the outstanding features of the equipment, or whatever the photograph is supposed to show.

Finally, always see that your literature is clean, and always handle it as though it were worth a lot of money . . . as though each sheet were printed on a five pound note. This creates the impression that not only is your literature worth reading, but you are obviously proud of what you are handling.

DEMONSTRATION

How convincing are you as a talker? Over luncheon at the Authors' Club, members were discussing the ability of various speakers, and some very fine speakers address the members of that Club. Someone said that he knew of only three good speakers. Another person mentioned that he knew a hundred bad ones. In the end we all decided that the number of good speakers in the country could be almost counted on a pair of hands. Not many salesmen are convincing speakers, but they have the advantage of being able to demonstrate.

Possibly they are only using pencil or paper, or they may just be showing a catalogue or booklet, but it does help them to talk fluently. If you don't believe this, try to explain any proposition you like to your wife, or to your friend. Don't use your hands, don't attempt to write anything and don't show anything. See what a job you have convincing them that what you are telling them is worth listening to.

If you are selling something at the moment which does not

lend itself to demonstration, then start again at the beginning of your sales sequence and introduce something into your story which will allow you to demonstrate.

Talking alone is not sufficient.

CAN YOU WRITE?

Smith is quite a good salesman but he's always moaning. He was with a firm selling disinfectants, and he groused all the time because they didn't spend enough money on advertising. Then he joined a firm selling machinery for moving crates and packages in store-rooms and factories. They advertised quite a lot and that pleased him. Soon, however, he started moaning that they didn't give him any good sales aids.

When he had been selling disinfectants he had a spray, he had various bottles of disinfectants with different aromas, and he had plenty of leaflets. "Now," he said to his sales manager, when he happened to be talking to him one day, "I miss that, you know. Demonstrating is half the battle, and you don't give me anything to demonstrate with."

The sales manager looked at Smith carefully and then said, "Smith, can you write?"

"Of course I can!" said Smith.

"Then what do you want demonstration models for?" asked the sales manager. "If a salesman can write he can give the best demonstration of all."

That sales manager was telling the truth. Often when you demonstrate a piece of machinery you interest the prospect, but it is far better to have the prospect working with you. The best kind of demonstration is when you and the customer or prospect are working *together*. Always have paper handy. Be ready with your pencil. And as soon as you discuss any selling point, bring out your pencil and start getting some figures down on to the paper.

"I'll show you what I mean, sir. If we can move ten crates in ten minutes, that will result in a time saving of . . ."

Write it all down. Make a mistake now and again, and check

up to see if the prospect is with you. If he spots the mistake, you may be sure that he is taking a great interest in what you're writing on that piece of paper.

THE 'WRITING-IT-DOWN' DEMONSTRATION IS ALWAYS WORTH USING.

PRACTISE

Let a conjuror fumble his trick and the slip is spotted pretty quickly. But few conjurors do make mistakes, because they rehearse and practise continuously, so that they are hand-perfect as well as word-perfect.

Too many salesmen do not realise how important it is to be able to demonstrate effectively. No salesman should attempt to demonstrate any article until he can carry out the demonstration almost blindfolded.

It's the same with selling literature. Every salesman should be able to produce a leaflet or catalogue without even looking into his case.

The conjuror who makes mistakes doesn't get any bookings. The salesman who mishandles his demonstrations loses sales.

CHAPTER XI

How to Handle Every Type of Buyer

THERE is something which every salesman has in common with his fellow salesmen, whatever they are selling. They are all meeting the same kind of customers.

This is how you can make customers—and then look after them.

HOW TO DEAL WITH TEN TOUGH CUSTOMERS

As a young man I was told that I had to handle people in the North Country differently from those in the South, and that West Country folk couldn't be tackled in the same manner as those in the East.

That is all nonsense. All buyers react to sales ideas in the same way. They all dislike certain types of salesmen for similar reasons; they buy for similar reasons; they refuse to buy for similar reasons. There are, however, some customers who are just a little tougher than others. They are the same at heart, but often they put over an act, either to frighten a salesman away, or to cover themselves if they decide not to buy. This is the way to tackle the various types who are hard to handle:

The Talker

He keeps on talking, and the salesman finds it difficult to get a word in edgeways. If the salesman feels that by letting the talker go on talking he is proving himself a good listener, he is wrong. Talkers can go on endlessly.

The salesman must be strong and, when confronted with a talker, must interrupt him at the first opportunity by using some sentence which the talker has used to bring out one of his sales points.

He could say something like this: "If you don't mind my interrupting for a moment, sir, what you have just said is so very right, because . . ." and then he must go on with his selling. He must continue to use this system until he has completed his whole sales story.

Too Friendly

Often the customer most difficult to sell to is the one who is too friendly. Beware of him, his friendship is often a guise, because he knows that by being friendly many salesmen are put off and are, therefore, not as insistent as they should be. They feel that they will upset the customer if, friendly as he is, they try to sell him too hard.

These tactics are the worst possible for this type of buyer. You can tell him that, because he is treating you so nicely, he should buy your products, because they will do his business the world of good. You must sell harder to the too friendly buyer than to anyone else.

The Snob

This type of customer is often the manager of a business, or the buyer. He is apt to look down on every type of salesman except his most intimate friends. He is suffering from a big inferiority complex.

Find something to praise about his work—his buying—his shop, and make him feel important. That's the only way to tackle him. If he gives you an inferiority complex and, because of this you try to show off, then you will never get the order.

The Frightened Buyer

This person is always scared of placing orders, although he has to do this all day long. He is so very afraid of making a mistake, especially if he is an employee.

The rule with this type of buyer is to tell him several verbal proof stories of how others have been successful with your goods. You should also undersell him, winning his confidence by telling him not to buy too much. When you have won his confidence he will no longer be frightened of you.

The Silent

The buyer who is silent is difficult to handle. He lets the salesman talk and talk until he has little more to say.

There are only two ways of dealing with this type of person: ask him questions and, more important still, ask his advice.

The Boaster

Never be misled by the boaster who talks in large quantities and tells you of the tremendous orders he has placed elsewhere. He is as scared at heart as is the frightened buyer.

Don't call his bluff. Don't try to get a big order because he talks only in large quantities. Just try for an average order. That will make him happy and, if you then tell him that you know full well that at later calls you will be one of the lucky ones who will be given a large order, you will please him immensely.

The Non-Listener

This type of man apparently doesn't listen to you at all, and often wanders away from you while you are talking to him.

Don't attempt to follow him, stand your ground. He will come back to you. Remember also to ask him questions, particularly about his own business. When he starts talking about his own business he will, eventually, start listening to what you have to say.

The Bluffer

This buyer is always trying to put you off, and eventually tells you that he will give you an order next time you call; or that he is not in the market at the moment, but he will certainly give you a chance at the first opportunity.

This only means that you haven't sold him well enough. Don't be bluffed. Improve your sales story and you will sell to him.

The Old Buyer

He may have been employed for thirty or forty years buying, or he may have been established in his own business for half a century or more. Because of this he has heard practically everything a salesman can tell him, and is inclined to be a little irritable on occasion.

He often upsets the young salesman, and many a young man has told me that he has felt at a distinct disadvantage when selling to this type of buyer. Some young men feel that the right way to tackle him is to show off, to prove that they know quite a lot about the business.

These tactics are wrong. Far better for the young salesman to appeal to this buyer's sense of fair play, admitting that he will never know as much about the trade as does the buyer, and ask for advice.

Women

Some women buyers are difficult to handle because they are governed by their likes and dislikes. Foolish flattery will not win them over. Being servile won't help at all.

The correct way to treat a woman buyer is to sell to her in exactly the same way as you would if she were a man. Remember another important point—you can sometimes make a mistake with a male buyer and he will forgive you. If you let a woman down she will remember it for ever. Be quite certain always to sell the right goods, therefore. Rather refuse an order than sell something which may remain on the shelves.

HOW TO GET MORE SALES

Few salesmen make sufficient use of their customers. On many occasions when I have mentioned this to a salesman I have been told that the time factor prohibits the spending of a lot of time with users. For example, if a salesman has to make nine or ten new calls a day he finds it very difficult to find time to call back on customers to nurse them, so that they in their turn will help to make other customers.

That's fair enough. But nursing a customer is rather different from looking after a customer. The latter is something which is expected of all salesmen. Every salesman worth his salt will do his best to look after his customers all the time, to see that they are satisfied and receiving good service. That isn't quite the same as spending hours nursing a customer along until he becomes very friendly towards a salesman and really wants to help him, as distinct from being asked to help him.

Now here is a way to increase your sales: branch out by creating branches. There are always some customers with whom you get on better than others. Spend all the time you can with these, restricting your calls on other customers to just a few minutes to make sure that they are still satisfied users.

Divide your territory up into a number of areas. If you cover a wide area, deal with each town separately.

Let us assume that you have thirty distinct areas in your territory. In each area you have a few customers, but what you want to do is to develop one special friend in each area—someone who is going to go right out of his way to help you. Whenever you come across such a customer, then really nurse him. Do more than you are entitled to do. Remember to find out when he has a birthday, and send him a birthday card. Find out details about his family. Drop him a line now and again. Send him a card while you are on holiday; send him a card at Christmas. Go out of your way to help him. If you do, you will find that eventually, in thirty different territories, you will have thirty friends who will, in fact, be the equivalent of your having thirty branches. Whenever you are in any particular district and you call upon your special customer he will greet you as a friend. He will tell you of others to call upon. He will give you leads, new sales angles and ideas.

This is one of the best methods of increasing sales, so remember to try to create a branch office for yourself in every area by cultivating firm friendships with those customers who are most friendly towards you.

KEEP IN THE NEWS

This is a motto which every salesman should remember: NEVER FORGET A CUSTOMER—NEVER LET A CUSTOMER FORGET YOU.

DISSATISFIED CUSTOMERS

A company selling specialised office equipment extracted statistics over a period of twelve months to find out why some customers were dissatisfied with their goods, or the service they had been given. Seventy per cent of the causes for complaint were traced back and attributed to salesmen—yes, to salesmen.

The amazing thing was that the salesmen who were complaining most that they had been let down were the very men who, themselves, had caused the dissatisfaction.

Here are a few basic reasons why the customers were dissatisfied:

(a) Salesmen not checking electric voltages, resulting in equipment being delivered which could not be operated.

(b) Salesmen promising delivery dates which could not be kept.

(c) Salesmen making claims for the equipment which could not be substantiated.

(d) Salesmen making off-the-record deals, and selling customers second-hand equipment to use in conjunction with the new appliances.

(e) Salesmen making promises to call back and look after the interests of their customers, and then forgetting to keep those promises.

If there are any dissatisfied customers in your area, don't grab your pen and write a sharp letter to your company. First make certain that you aren't the cause of the complaint.

FEW DEAD PROSPECTS

"It's a waste of time," said Smith to his sales manager, "to call on Barter & Barter again. I must have called on them at least thirty times. I can't do anything with them."

"If that's the way you feel about it," answered the sales manager, "then I want to make a suggestion to you. Your territory is guaranteed, therefore no one else is allowed to call on your customers. But would you allow me to send another salesman to your territory to call on those half-dozen prospects where you've been calling for months now—in one case for years—without getting any results whatsoever?"

Smith looked a bit wary about this. No man likes giving up his territory, even if he does think it isn't any good. However, having been forced into a corner he couldn't do anything else but say, "If you want to try it, you can. It'll be a sheer waste of time. . . ."

Would it be a waste of time? That is not a record of an actual conversation which I have heard taking place, but I am quite certain that if it were to take place a lot of good would come of it.

Every sales manager running a speciality organisation could tell stories of impossible prospects who were later sold by other salesmen, but the same applies to staple goods as well. One salesman will call at a shop for years with no result, until he gives up the prospect as hopeless. Then he retires from the territory and along comes another salesman who opens the account.

Selling isn't only a matter of explaining one's products. Most salesmen have heard the old saying, *he didn't sell because his face didn't fit.* My advice to salesmen is not to let other men go to their territory to turn prospects into customers, but if their 'face doesn't fit' with certain prospects they should find out why. Possibly they have irritated those prospects, acted condescendingly towards them, or upset them in some other way. If you have a prospect like that don't try to force him to buy anything; don't talk too much about your goods, but call again. Sell yourself as hard as you can. Try to do him a service.

Another point—don't take your customer for granted. Do you ever read the 'Advice on Marriage' columns in the papers? If you do you will find that invariably there will be a letter from a distracted wife asking what she should do about her husband, who no longer shows affection. Usually it will be written on these lines: *At one time he used to kiss me goodbye every morning, and once a week he would bring me flowers. Now we've been married about five years and he sometimes forgets to kiss me goodbye and rarely brings home any flowers for me. What should I do about it?*

I'm not in a position to give advice to newlyweds, but if the authority on marriage were to have a chat with the husband concerned, he would probably say to him, "The trouble with you is that you're taking your wife too much for granted."

Unfortunately, most married men do that after a time. They forget all those little courtesies they indulged in when they were first married, which made their wives so happy.

Salesmen often act in a similar way towards their customers. When first they open an account they are polite, they do everything possible to see that the customer is satisfied, they try to help him by explaining the benefits of their goods and how those benefits will help him, and so on. Then a few years pass, and the salesman takes his customer for granted. He doesn't sell nearly so well when he calls. He is not nearly so alert with his sales talk. He tells a joke or two, and thinks this takes the place of strong selling.

Oh, yes, he still gets an order from his customer, he still thinks he's well in because he's doing just a little bit more business than he did when first he opened the account.

If salesmen would always remember, however, not to take their customers for granted, but to sell just as hard after they have been calling on them for five years as they did when they first called, they would get many more orders.

MAKING IT STICK

Watching a television show I heard a recipe for success which was given by a successful business man to interviewer

Michael Parkinson. He said, "I have always taken good care to fight my reverses. My successes can look after themselves."

I couldn't help thinking at the time about the reverses which come to a salesman during his years on the road. Some of them come about through no fault of his own. Others he could fight, or avoid altogether. I suppose the types of reverse which a salesman dislikes most are those which announce themselves in a commission statement by way of a debit against commission. They usually mean that an order has been cancelled.

Everyone who has ever sold anything has had a cancellation at some time. I must admit that I never got used to going back to a customer to try and talk him into rescinding his cancellation and making it a firm order once more. Sometimes the cancellation has occurred through no fault of the salesman. The customer may have suffered a sudden financial loss, or illness may have come to him.

But that is not the usual cause of a cancellation. What generally happens is that a salesman doesn't sell sufficiently hard on what his product will do for the prospect. He makes a sale because of his strong personality but, once he has left the customer's premises, the personality is forgotten and the purchase remembered. Then the customer becomes worried, probably consults his wife or some other member of the firm, thinks he has made a mistake and promptly sends through a cancellation.

To avoid cancellations, make a complete sale at every call. There is a school of thought which says, *get the order when you can*, which means that after a few minutes with the prospect, if he shows interest, get him signed up quickly.

I don't agree with that. If you can obtain an order quickly by all means do so, but then cement confidence by explaining to the prospect what your goods will do for him.

A salesman's job is to make his customers feel that they have exercised really sound judgment in placing their order. This enhances their ego, and after that they will rarely cancel.

Salesmen selling staple goods, who know their customers well, are also sometimes faced with this troublesome cancellation business. After they have left their friend's premises, he may decide that he is overstocked after all, and because he feels that the salesman is a friend he considers that he is entitled to cancel his order—one more reason why the commercial traveller who calls regularly on his customers should never develop into just a goodwill worker. If he sells his products on every call, regardless of whether he calls once a week or once a year, or whether he's known his prospect or customer for one year or ten, then he won't be troubled with cancellations.

The best way of fighting reverses is not to have them. To avoid cancellations, make certain that your customer fully understands what you are selling to him and what he is buying before you leave his premises, and spend a minute or two cementing confidence.

ACCURACY COUNTS

It has often been said that a salesman should meet his customers' requirements accurately. True enough. But it applies more to the speciality salesman than to the man selling staple goods.

Many salesmen selling staples call upon their friends in the trade week after week, month after month, and almost make up the order before they call. They know exactly what is going to be bought. In doing this they often overlook the possibilities of extra sales, resulting from different sales promotion methods or extra drive.

I have seen so many cases of retailers increasing their sales of certain commodities because of a sales brainwave or a new idea that I would hesitate to advise any staple salesman to be sure that he had assessed accurately the customers' requirements at every call.

The salesman selling specialities is placed in a different category. Too many speciality salesmen are price-conscious. They may be selling printing machines, weighing machines, cash registers, fire extinguishers or what you will, but on many occasions they don't even attempt accurately to gauge the requirements of their customers; they just want to sell them something, and because of that they sometimes have a dis-satisfied customer.

If a building requires eighty fire extinguishers to give it full protection, then the salesman should sell eighty. If, when selling air-conditioning equipment, a thousand pounds' worth of unit equipment is necessary to deal with a room, then the salesman should sell that thousand pounds' worth of equipment or refuse the order.

That is what is meant by saying that a salesman should always see that he does meet his customers' requirements accurately. If he undersells he will have a dissatisfied customer. If he oversells, then he is unfair to his customer, and the end will be the same.

Be a 'made to measure' salesman, and sell the right equipment, *accurately*, all the time.

RUMOUR CAN KILL A BUSINESS

We all know the power of suggestion, and we all know that once a suggestion has been put into the mind it is hard to eradicate. Some years ago, when I was changing an old model car for a new vehicle, I was thinking of buying a model X. Somebody said to me, "Oh, I shouldn't touch it at any price. They're high-revving engines—they'll wear themselves out in a few thousand miles. That car's built for show."

I never did buy a model X. Often I have been near to buying it, but whenever I have almost made up my mind I have remembered those few words about the engine, and the suggestion was so strong that I didn't buy.

There are very few motorists who have not, at some time or another, been told that a certain make of car isn't as good as it ought to be. And very rarely do those motorists ever buy that make of car.

That will show you the power of rumour. Obviously the man who first told me about this had been badly treated by the dealers of the X car. He had a grudge against them, and from then onwards he told everybody that the engines were of little use.

Yes, rumours, if they can't kill a business, can do a great deal of harm. And that is one of the reasons why salesmen should go to endless trouble to see that they do satisfy their customers.

Never let a customer spread bad rumours about your products.

RARELY TWO AT A TIME

In racing it is quite hard to pull off a double. It's just as hard in salesmanship. A salesman may pull off a very big order on Monday morning. He only needs another one like it to give him the biggest week he has ever had—yet, somehow, that other outsize order eludes him. He may get it two or three weeks later, but it always seems impossible to get it during the same week.

It's the same with pet customers. The majority of salesmen selling staple goods have one customer who really looks upon his firm as his main supplier. The salesman is always confident of getting good results at every call he makes upon that customer. Then there comes a time when he gradually works his way into the goodwill of another store and they place large orders with him. What happens then, more often than not, is that the first customer, who was always the standby, drops out. The buyer changes his job, or something like that happens. Fate seems always to be playing this kind of trick on salesmen.

What it all adds up to is that if a salesman does his job thoroughly and properly, day in and day out, month in and month out, the law of averages will always operate in his favour. By the law of averages some customers will drop out and cease to buy from a company, and others will place initial orders and become regular buyers.

So far as building up new trade goes, however, the law of averages can only work if the salesman does everything possible to increase his number of customers. The average firm loses fifteen per cent of customers every year. Do you realise what that means? Fifteen per cent of your customers will drop out by the end of this year. Now what are you going to do to replace them? The good salesman, while doing everything he can to retain the goodwill of his customers, always has it in his mind that he may lose them one day. As they must be replaced by others, he has continually to make new calls, so that the number of new customers he makes each year is always slightly greater than the number of old ones he loses.

CHAPTER XII

Forty Ideas for Increasing Sales

ALTHOUGH a salesman may be working in the right way, may have a good sales sequence, and may understand human relations, he can still do even more to increase sales. Here are some ideas to help salesmen obtain more orders.

IT MEANS EVERYTHING

The speaker raised his arm, clenched his fist, glared around the room, then let his face break into a smile. I guessed what was coming.

"You gotta have it," said the speaker. He shouted, "You gotta have it! Do you hear me, you gotta have it." We couldn't help hearing him. He had a microphone, and his voice bellowed through the room.

It was at a sales meeting in New York in 1948.

"You know what you gotta have?" he almost screamed. "Let's hear it from you."

Back came the cry: "Enthusiasm!"

Yes, they were a well-trained audience of salesmen listening to their sales manager giving one of his weekly sales talks.

"Come on," shouted the sales manager, "let's give it to 'em. After me—let's burn 'em up! Let's burn 'em up! Let's burn 'em up!"

And the audience went into their chant: "Let's burn 'em up! Let's burn 'em up! Let's burn 'em up!"

I was not quite sure who was going to be burned up, but I assumed that it meant the audience's prospects and customers were really going to be treated with burning enthusiasm during the next few days. Anyway, I thoroughly enjoyed the meeting, although it was a little different from the one I had attended in London some months earlier. On this occasion the sales manager hadn't thrown his hands into the air, he hadn't shouted, but he had said quietly and forcefully, "Gentlemen, you cannot sell successfully without enthusiasm." And although we hadn't then sung, "Let's burn 'em up", we had all agreed with the sales manager.

I don't think I have ever read a book on salesmanship which has not stressed the fact that, unless a man is a red-hot enthusiast, he will not make a successful salesman. And, of course, that is true. In fact, if I had a magic lamp similar to the one used by Aladdin, and the Genie would grant me only one wish for every salesman who called to see me, I shouldn't wish for the salesman to be a hard worker, or that he should be able to learn a sales sequence, or that he should know how to answer objections or that he should understand human relations. I should have just one wish—LET HIM BE ENTHUSIASTIC.

REMEMBER, ENTHUSIASM IS NOT HALF THE BATTLE, IT IS VICTORY BEFORE THE BATTLE STARTS.

STICKABILITY

How does an umpire count the number of balls in an over? As he doesn't want to look foolish by allowing a bowler to have a seven-ball over, to make certain that he is counting correctly he usually has six coins in one pocket, and, each time a ball is bowled, he transfers one coin to another pocket. When the six have been used up he calls "Over".

It might be a good thing for a salesman if every sale were umpired, with the umpire calling "Out!" when he realises that the salesman has finished his effort. Most salesmen give up far too quickly.

Whatever we want from life has to be fought for, and that includes orders. If you want a decision on the spot you will be well advised to copy the umpire. Have six coins in your pocket. Every time you get a "No!" transfer a coin to another pocket and then go on selling. Never give yourself "Out!" before you have transferred all six coins.

TO SUCCEED, A SALESMAN MUST BE ABLE TO DEVELOP STICK-ABILITY WITHOUT ANTAGONISING THE BUYER.

SELL AN EXTRA

This has probably happened to you. If it hasn't, then you can check it yourself. Go into the nearest menswear shop to buy some cufflinks. It won't cost you much, but it will teach you a fine lesson.

You will probably come out of that shop with only the cufflinks, and the assistant won't have tried to sell you anything else. Or, if he has mentioned other articles, he will have gabbled so rapidly that he might just as well have kept quiet. For example, "Would you like any ties, socks, shirts, hats? . . ." And as you are not really listening to him you only buy your cufflinks.

Thousands of pounds a day could be added to the retail turnover of this country if only retail salesmen were to improve their salesmanship.

Don't think I'm blaming the salesmen—I am not. I blame the managers and owners of the businesses who don't go to the trouble of training their salesmen sufficiently.

I read in a trade paper that customers couldn't expect superservice from assistants in one certain trade, as they couldn't be paid well enough because of restrictions of profit in that trade. That, of course, is a poor argument. If the assistants were better trained and were to sell more, then obviously they could be paid more.

I proved this to a retailer the other day when he disagreed with me. He was a chemist who had a good local trade, and knew most of his customers. He had just received a delivery of a new line in nylon toothbrushes. I asked him if he had confidence in them, and he said they were the best in the world. I said to him, "Why don't you tell that to every customer who comes in this morning?"

Out of twenty customers approached in this way, four purchased brushes. Extras can always be sold if they are singled out for sale. The same applies to many salesmen who have accessories to their main articles of sale. Here is another example:

One of my companies sells air-conditioning equipment. Some

of the units contain air filters. These are supplied with the units, and replacements are quite inexpensive—so inexpensive, in fact, that there is very little commission for the salesmen and, therefore, many of them don't bother to talk about spare filters.

One month we started a drive and suggested to every salesman that he should ask each customer to buy a spare filter. The company employs over a hundred salesmen, and the result of this drive was the extra sale of thousands of filters.

Remember, the good salesman always tries to sell extras.

THE LITTLE 'UNS COUNT

A student came to see us the other day to ask us to help him increase sales. He had just started selling to grocers, and he brought with him a list of his accounts. On going through the accounts he pointed out one or two of them with whom he was doing very good business, while of others he said, "They're quite small accounts."

This is the suggestion I made: "Try turning your small accounts into big accounts. Every salesman has to find new customers—you don't need us to tell you that. But too many salesmen take it for granted that because a shopkeeper has always been a small buyer he must forever give small orders. It's surprising the quantity of goods that so-called small firms can buy, and the fact that they are not buying much from you means that you are not selling them properly."

Do your best to turn every small account into a large account—that's the way to increase business.

WHY THERE'S A CARDBOARD SHORTAGE

Someone said recently that if every piece of showcard not being used by retailers were collected, a bonfire could be lit which would burn for months and months. That is an exaggeration, perhaps, but there must be tons of cardboard lying idle—not just plain cardboard either, but coloured board with interesting designs and varying shapes, the brain children of sales managers and advertising experts. Firms spend thousands of pounds on display material of this kind, and it is believed that over eighty per cent is never used, whilst out of the twenty per cent remaining five per cent is used so badly as to be ineffectual.

Shopkeepers are, of course, inundated with display material, and they only use the particular items which appeal to them at a given time. The reason why the display material is not more widely used, however, is because salesmen don't take any trouble to help their customers, and some firms send out such inferior material that it wouldn't be used anyway.

Here is a rule for salesmen : if your company provides display aids for your customers, then it's up to you to see that they are properly used. See that the showcard is near a cash desk, or on a busy counter. Try to have it placed between waist level and eye level. Sell your customers on the idea of using the aids, not for your benefit, but for their own benefit. Sell your display material as you sell your goods, because by doing this your display material will help to sell more goods for you.

IDEAS UNLIMITED

Too many salesmen take everything for granted. They criticise many of their firm's ideas without being at all constructive. Also, too many salesmen stagnate.

The way to overcome both these defects is to try to develop a new sales idea every day. Although, possibly, only one of the ideas every month will be really workable, that idea should compensate you for the great thought that you have given to your job.

New ideas create new sales but, more than that, they increase a man's self-esteem.

MAKE IT FIT

A firm selling a specialised type of oil for cars tried selling the oil to garages, so that they in turn would sell the product to their customers. Many garage owners couldn't see that their customers would spend money on this 'extra'. Then the firm hit upon the idea of getting their salesmen to sell the oil *for* the garages.

They trained their salesmen to call upon local users and take an order for the oil—but not in the name of the company manufacturing the product—in the name of the local garage. The salesmen then called upon the local garage proprietor and said, "Look, sir, I've got these orders for you. We don't supply direct, so we'll invoice to you and you can resell and take the profit." Then he would add, "I've found you customers, and there are many more like them. You only have to stock our oil and it will be additional business for you."

Naturally, garage proprietors were always pleased to receive extra business without any effort and, in the majority of cases, they placed orders for stock.

Now what were that firm doing? They were remembering a golden rule of selling—FIT YOUR PRODUCT INTO THE PROSPECT'S BUSINESS. Don't expect him to try to alter his business to fit your product.

DON'T BE THANKFUL FOR SMALL MERCIES

The salesman came out of the office beaming all over. His area manager was waiting for him outside. "I can see the result," he said, "what did you sell?"

The salesman gave a sigh of relief as he said, "I got a ten thousand pound life policy. What do you think of that?"

"That's good!" said the area manager. "But didn't you sell him an accident policy as well?"

That area manager was right. He should, of course, have praised the salesman a little more before telling him about the accident policy, but he was reminding the salesman that he hadn't sold enough.

Too many salesmen take an order for a gross of coat-hangers, or a dozen model dresses, or a piece of material, and they are so delighted to get that one order that they forget that their prospect, while he was in a buying mood, might have bought other articles as well.

Don't be too elated when you get an order. Quieten yourself down and, having got it, try to sell the prospect something else.

Most salesmen could add twenty per cent to their turnover each year if they decided to become heartily dissatisfied with whatever order they obtained.

ALWAYS TRY TO SELL MORE.

DEVELOPING SALES IDEAS FOR SALES AIDS

Some salesmen demonstrate machines, some show samples, others handle catalogues. Speciality salesmen usually have specialised sales aids.

Whether a salesman carries a sample or not, he usually relies on a sales aid of some kind or another. Often, sales managers let their salesmen carry on year after year using the same sales aids, when these could be improved. This is how you can go about checking *your* sales aids, to see if you can improve them:

1. *Make them larger, or make them smaller*. Sometimes a sales aid, when reduced to a miniature, can be more effective than one of standard size. At other times, if it is made on a large scale it will attract more attention.

2. *Study the sales aids used for other products*—products entirely different from the one you are selling. You will often find that they will give you an idea which you can ally to your own sales aids.

3. *Join two ideas together*. You may have two separate sales aids, both quite useful in themselves which, if used together, become much stronger.

4. *Try to alter your sales aids* so that your customers will be able to participate in their use. Can they check up on

something for themselves? Can they help them to analyse their own sales? Get your customers to work with you.

5. *Light it up.* Have you a sales aid which could be lit up by incorporating a battery and a lamp?

6. *Study all newspaper advertisements.* Advertisements can often give you a new angle for your own sales aids.

YOU MUST KEEP TRYING TO IMPROVE YOUR SALES TOOLS.

ARE ALL BLONDES DUMB?

I think it all began with Anita Loos who, you may remember, wrote a book about blondes—and very dumb blondes they were at that! I don't know whether blondes are more dumb than brunettes, but I do know that some salesmen are very dumb. When making a sale the trouble really begins with the salesman's eagerness to keep on talking. Because of this he not only loses his power of observation but, also, apparently, he needs a deaf aid.

The professional salesman listens for little things. The big statements, the main objections, he takes in his stride—he expects them. So does the average salesman for that matter. But the professional salesman makes capital out of the phrases which are sometimes almost whispered. Phrases such as:

"*Yes, I think Binks had one—they were quite happy.*"
"*It wants something to smarten up those garage hands.*"
"*I read something about it in the paper the other day.*"
"*Does it go with the decorations?*"
"*Is it heavy to handle?*"

The average salesman hears those sentences, gabbles something in agreement, and goes on with his sales story.

The professional salesman stops for a moment (whatever point he is trying to make) when he hears such sentences, because he knows what has happened. For example, if the sentence is, "Does it go with the decorations?" he then makes tremendous play on how the equipment has been specially designed to match all kinds of decorations. Then he refers to the prospect's own building and how the equipment might have been specially designed for that very building, and so on.

The professional salesman does that because he realises that those sentences are not just ordinary phrases—they are BUYING SIGNALS. So listen for those buying signals. Listen carefully for them, and whenever you hear one you will know that you are not only half-way towards your sale, but you have a major point to elaborate. Don't treat it lightly. *Treat it as an important issue.* MORE SALES HAVE BEEN LOST THROUGH IGNORING BUYING SIGNALS than almost anything else—AND MORE SALES HAVE BEEN GAINED QUICKLY BY LISTENING FOR THEM.

DON'T SELL HIM ONE

There is a certain bookstall which regularly displays several copies of one book. The manager of this bookstall has told me that on many occasions this has resulted in a far greater turnover than he used to achieve when he displayed a number of different books. Obviously, therefore, if this manager is interested in a book and will give it a full display, a salesman who sells him on the idea of making the show will benefit.

Just as obviously, any salesman who called on that manager would do his best to sell him a quantity of books to enable the show to be made, rather than take an order for just one or two books which could not be shown to the best advantage.

This does prove a point—that when a buyer orders a quantity of anything he will usually make a display of it, whereas when he buys a small amount and hopes there will be a demand for the goods often this does not occur.

Every shopkeeper has his shelves stocked with items which he may have had in stock for some time, and which have not sold for one reason only—because he has not shown them to anyone. Salesmen who sell to retailers have told me that it is a bad mistake to oversell a buyer, because when they call back next time they find that they have lost his confidence. It can be maintained just as well that to undersell a buyer is an equally certain method of losing his confidence. On the next visit of the salesman who has only sold one or two of his articles to a shop-keeper, unless he is extremely lucky, he will be met with, "I still have them on my shelf, so I can't buy any more just now." Every salesman, therefore, should rather err slightly by over-selling than by underselling.

If a salesman wishes to oversell grossly and load the retailer up with his goods, then of course he is making a big mistake, unless he is prepared to do something to help the retailer shift his stock. The rule, therefore, should always be:

TRY TO OVERSELL JUST A LITTLE AND, BY DOING SO, YOU WILL GET YOUR GOODS DISPLAYED AND STAND A BETTER CHANCE OF REPEAT BUSINESS.

EIGHT WAYS OF HELPING A PROSPECT

Have you ever considered that when you are making a sale the prospect has to work quite hard as well? In selling, it isn't always a good thing to study the other man's point of view, but a salesman should be conscious of what a prospect has to do while a sale is taking place.

1. He has to listen to you.
2. He has to judge your proposition while you are talking.
3. He must form an opinion of your organisation.
4. He must ask questions where he is not clear about any point.
5. He has to consider the advantages to himself of placing an order with you.
6. He must bring to mind any possible objections.
7. He has to arrive at a decision.
8. Having arrived at a decision he has to place the order.

Now if you help the prospect to do his job you will be selling correctly. So study these points and, when next you make a sale, realise what the prospect has to do, and encourage him to develop these eight points. Remember that when you know the lines on which the prospect is thinking you are already half-way towards supplying the correct answers.

SELL 'EM ALL

It's surprising the number of people there are in an organisation who can put a stop to an order being placed. A simple example would be the small shop owned by a husband and wife. A salesman might sell to the husband and be about to get a good order. The wife may then come into the shop, hear just a part of the conversation, and tell her husband that she doesn't think he ought to buy.

Taking it a stage further, you may have a husband and a wife in the shop and one assistant. The salesman, wisely, may sell to the husband and wife, and they may both think that an order should be placed. Then perhaps the husband will call over to his assistant, "Charlie, are you all right for XYZ soap?"

Charlie may reply, "We haven't any in stock, but you remember when we tried it about six months ago it didn't go at all."

That can kill an order.

When we think of a factory and all the executives and minor executives employed in a factory who can stop a sale materialising, then we realise just how carefully the salesman must plan his effort.

He may be selling to a general manager and his sale can be blocked by the welfare manageress. Perhaps he's selling to the canteen manager and the sale is blocked by the cook. A sale to the factory manager can be put off by a foreman in the works.

Whatever you are selling, try to find out all the people who could be implicated in the sale, and then do your very best to get them on your side. Although it is a standard rule in selling that the salesman should not waste time, but should always sell to the man who is able to sign the order, it is never a waste of time to spend a few minutes with a shop assistant, a foreman, a waiter in a restaurant, or anyone else who can help to get him the order, or who at any rate, if not able to help him, will not block the sale at the last minute.

WON'T KEEP YOU A MINUTE

"One of the difficulties," says John Morgan, "of selling life insurance to busy executives is to get them to give you sufficient time to tell your story. Not every insurance man can sell over a good lunch or at the golf club bar. It is usually necessary to see the executive in his own office. Salesmen are taught," insists Morgan, "that when they ask for five minutes of a prospect's time they should do so with the knowledge that if they are interesting enough the prospect will often let the salesman stay longer.

"When I tie myself down to a time," he said, "after it is up I say to the prospect, 'That, in brief, is what I can do for you. I said that I would not keep you more than five minutes, and my time is up. If I have interested you sufficiently and you want to hear more and you would like me to stay, then, of course, I shall be happy to do so. But if you would prefer me to go away I'll leave right now.' On nearly every occasion the prospect allows me to continue, because he feels that I have not tried to outstay my welcome."

BUY VERSUS SELL

Butchers used to sell off their stock cheaply every week-end. "Buy! Buy! Buy!" they would shout, hoping to entice passers-by into their shop to make a purchase.

That was all right for its purpose, but too many salesmen think in terms of buying instead of in terms of selling. Unless you are selling capital equipment or a service, you are selling, in the main, goods for resale. If you sell to a wholesaler, although you may be able to give him a hundred reasons, he wants just one reason to tell him how he can sell your goods. He has to resell them.

The same applies to a retailer. He doesn't want to be told that he should buy ten pieces of material because they are

beautifully designed. He wants to know how he can sell those
ten pieces of material. When the salesman is thinking in terms
of buying, and the prospect is thinking in terms of selling, their
ideas are poles apart.

Whenever a salesman is dealing with a wholesaler, or with
any other type of buyer who has to resell his goods, he should
think in terms of how the prospect can sell his products. He
should work out in advance what features of his goods the
retailer or the wholesaler can use to enable them to sell more.
Then, when he calls, he will not talk in terms of buying, he will
talk in terms of the other man's selling.

MAKE THEM WANT IT

It is said of Lord Duveen, the greatest salesman of paintings
the world has ever known, that it was most difficult to buy from
him. He never seemed anxious to sell anything—there always
seemed to be a dozen reasons why he couldn't let someone have
a particular painting.

This attitude on his part made his clients all the more
anxious to pay the fabulous prices that he asked for his Rem-
brandts, his Gainsboroughs, his Renoirs, etc.

His selling methods are well worth copying. Whenever you
appear too anxious to sell, you never get the order. Never give
your customer the feeling that the only thing you want to do at
that particular time is to sell him something. When you make
him feel that you are not too anxious to take his order then you
stand a better chance of getting it.

DON'T BE A STOPPER

Salesmen are taught to analyse every sale in which they take
part which doesn't result in an order. Most men do try to do
this. They endeavour to find out why they didn't get the sale.
Many, however, don't go about it the right way.

Fred Dixon, who trains salesmen to sell recording machines,
put it this way:

"If you don't get an order, don't go through a complicated formula, analysing your mistakes. Ask yourself this question: *What did I do to stop the prospect buying?* If you didn't get the order, you were the man who actually stopped that prospect from signing your order form. You stopped him buying, because you didn't know every one of your sales points or, if you did know them, you didn't put them over with sufficient conviction. Possibly, you stopped him buying because you didn't point out why your machines were worth more money than those of your competitors. Perhaps you stopped him because you didn't sell with integrity, or you didn't create confidence."

The next time you don't get an order just ask yourself this question: *How did I stop that prospect from placing his order with me?*

ON BEING BROKE

Sometimes, if you talk to well-to-do business men, you get the impression that the only happy days of their lives were when they were really hard up. I think that is nonsense. When we are really broke we are never very happy although, in later years when we look back, we try to kid ourselves that things weren't so bad, so that we do then honestly believe that we had some degree of happiness, in spite of our lack of capital.

The only advantage of being hard up is that it does teach us something. We learn facts about life which cannot be learned in any other way.

I remember many years ago when I was selling shopfronts. I was hard up, and I wasn't being too successful, and I was working on a straight commission basis. One day I called on a shop in Bedfordshire. I started my sales story and suddenly realised that I was getting interest. My sales aid was a very well-designed booklet giving suggestions for different types of shop-front. They ranged, in those days, from a few hundred to a few thousand pounds.

I talked about a fascia costing about two hundred and fifty pounds. The prospect took the catalogue away from me, glanced through the pages, and stopped at a design costing approximately fifteen hundred pounds.

"I don't think that is the type of fascia that will interest you," I said, and back I went to my two-hundred-and-fifty-pound job, driving home my sales points one after the other.

He listened to me for some few minutes. Then he said, "What's the price of the other one?"

"Which other one?" I asked.

"The one I was looking at before."

"Oh, that!" I said. "It's about fifteen hundred pounds. But I think this is all you need here. This is what you really want. . . ."

The man staggered me by saying, "No, I'll have the fifteen-hundred-pound design."

I could hardly believe my ears. In fact, I thought he was pulling my leg. I'm afraid it took him some little time to convince me that he meant what he said.

I took the order and, from then on, things went well with me. The reason why he wanted such an elaborate fascia was because some little way down the road one of his rivals had altered his premises, and he wanted to do something better. As he had quite a small shop I didn't think he was in a position to pay fifteen hundred pounds, but in point of fact he was an extremely wealthy man, owning a lot of property in the area.

Where had I gone wrong? I had judged the prospect's pocketbook by the size of my own. I was broke, so I couldn't imagine anyone spending more than two hundred pounds at the most. I hadn't thought of his needs or his requirements, or of what he wanted. I had thought of the whole sale in terms of hard cash.

Every salesman has his good times and his bad, and it is during his bad times that he must guard most carefully against believing that his prospects or his customers are as hard up as he is.

When a prospect tells him that money's tight he may only be using it as a figure of speech. In point of fact, he may have a very big bank balance, and be ready to place a big order.

CHAPTER XIII

Twenty-Six Ways a Field Manager Can Help His Salesmen

MORE often than not the first promotion a salesman achieves is to that of field manager. There are, of course, various grades of field management—inspectors, supervisors, area managers or district managers. The title doesn't matter a lot, because the function remains the same. A field manager has to work with his men, and help them to sell more.

A good supervisor can greatly increase the turnover of his salesmen. If, however, he does not do his job properly, he can do more harm than good.

TOUGH, BUT KINDLY

It goes without saying that a field manager must thoroughly understand human relations. That means that he must be able to see the other man's point of view. He must be man enough to apologise if he makes a mistake. He must not boast or brag. He must do his best to make the other man feel important; and he must be lavish with his praise, and sparing with his criticism.

A most important aspect of human relations, however, applies to some managers—particularly those newly appointed to the position. They feel that it is incumbent upon them to show their authority, or to give orders. The good manager should never have to do this. It should be his ideal to prove to his men that he is so worthy of their trust and friendship that they will do everything for him without being driven by commands.

A manager must never say, "I order you to do this . . ." or "You must do that . . ." unless a salesman has committed a grave misdemeanour. And then, of course, it would hardly be necessary, because the salesman would be dismissed from the company.

Remember then:

Never try to show your authority;
Never throw your weight about;
Never boast of orders you have taken in the past;
Never boast of your achievements;
BE MODEST AT ALL TIMES, AND LET YOUR ACTIONS SPEAK FOR YOU.

Obviously, at certain times salesmen have to be reprimanded because they make mistakes. Even so, this can be done in a kindly manner.

I have met many boasters, and 'tick-em-off' boys who, at heart, were really very weak men. The strong man is the man who can get things done *because* of his kindly manner, and because of the fact that others, knowing that he is really strong, would never attempt to take advantage of his kindnesses.

SET HIM AN EXAMPLE

The district manager of quite a well-known company called at my office. It didn't look as though he had changed his collar for two or three days, his shoes were certainly not clean, and his finger-nails were grubby.

What a bad example for his men! How could he expect them to take a pride in their appearance, when he was so untidy?

Of just as much importance as appearance is punctuality. There is no excuse for the field manager being late for an appointment with one of his salesmen. It doesn't matter if he has to get up at five in the morning, he must still be the first to arrive—to set an example.

How's your language? I don't mean can you speak French or Spanish. I mean do you use bad language?

Most men swear on occasion, and if it's mild it doesn't do much harm. But what may be mild swearing to one man can be hard swearing to another. It is best, therefore, for a field manager not to use bad language in front of a salesman.

So be careful to

Check your appearance;
Always be punctual;
Watch your language.

GOSSIP

A field manager must never run down other salesmen with whom he has worked. He must never talk about their sales, unless it will help the salesman with whom he is working to do better. He must not talk about their customers, their prospects, or what business they are doing. He must concentrate on the man he is with.

MEETING A SALESMAN

There is one vital point a supervisor must remember when he meets a salesman:

WHEN HE WALKS TOWARDS HIM, HE MUST SMILE.

BE DYNAMIC

When meeting a new salesman, many field managers have told me that it is their usual practice to have coffee together first, so that they can have a chat, and the field manager can find out something about the salesman's back-ground.

What a waste of time! He can find out all the background he wants to during the walking that takes place in between calls.

There is only one way to greet a new salesman—a smiling welcome, and then, "Let's start work."

The speciality field manager should take his salesman into the nearest shop or office, and start selling. The field manager selling staple goods should make straight for the nearest customer—or better still, try to open a new account right away.

That is being dynamic, and salesmen like dynamic field managers.

If you insist upon having your chat before you start working, then the answer is simple. Instead of meeting a salesman at nine o'clock (if that is your usual meeting time), arrange to meet him at eight o'clock, and have your coffee until eight-thirty. Then start work.

DON'T BE DIFFERENT

Some supervisors feel proud of the fact that their sales kit is really superb. They have begged or borrowed from head office all sorts of things to help the sale along. They have accumulated much over the years.

That's fair enough, so long as they are working on their own. But when working with a salesman nearly everything in their kit which the salesman hasn't got must be discarded. The field manager must use the same sales aids as his salesman.

The only exception to this may be a sales aid which the field manager has made himself, and which the salesman could make if he cared to take the trouble. For example, it could be a press-cutting book, or a booklet showing various advertisements which the firm have used.

And talking about kits, remember this: Whether you are working with a new salesman or an old-timer, it is your duty to check his kit on each occasion that you work with him, and if it is not in good condition and clean and tidy, it's up to you, in a friendly manner, to try to get him to mend his ways.

THE TRAVELLERS' GRAVEYARD

You already know that the average salesman never appreciates his territory. On many occasions you will be met by salesmen who will tell you that their territory is the world's worst. Earlier in this book you will have read how to tackle this problem, and you may like to mention the proof which I have given in the shape of letters from all over the country from salesmen complaining about their territories.

There is one thing you must never do, and that is to sympathise with a salesman regarding his area. You must never allow him to think for one moment that there is anything wrong with his territory. If you agree with him on this question you are going to cause a lot of concern at head office—and when head office have a lot of worry they don't like the man who causes it.

The best way to prove to a salesman that his territory is as good as any other is to go out and SELL ON IT.

MEETINGS

The new manager invariably wants to arrange regular meetings with his salesmen. I do not consider these meetings necessary. It is far better to deal with salesmen individually than collectively.

If all the salesmen are doing well, then there is no harm in a meeting. But if a few members of the team are having a lean patch, then they affect the other salesmen, and the meeting develops into a 'moan session'.

Many a good man has been lost through attending such meetings.

NO THANKS!

Shakespeare was quite right! There is nothing so unkind as man's ingratitude. The best thing for a field manager to do, therefore, is not to expect any gratitude, and then he won't be disappointed.

You would think that if you obtain a big order for a salesman he would be grateful. You would think that if you increase an order for staple goods substantially, the salesman would again be grateful.

Not a bit of it! He is glad to get the order, of course, but not so thankful as you would think. He feels slightly hurt at the fact that you obtained the order which he hadn't pulled off, and he is worried about what head office will think. So don't worry if the salesman doesn't thank you profusely for what you have done for him.

Do your job properly, and you will impress your head office—and they are the only people you want to impress.

WHO TALKS?

It is not easy for two people to take part in a sale. The best plan for the field manager, if he is working with a salesman for three days, is for him to do all the selling on the first day; the salesman on the second day; and to try to make it a joint effort on the third day.

If you are only with a salesman for one day and you are selling staple goods, then again, you should make all the running for the morning, and let the salesman make the running in the afternoon.

He must do this to enable you to help him improve his sales story.

DO MORE

You must do more than the salesman can expect you to do. If a salesman starts work at nine in the morning, then you must insist on starting work at eight-thirty. If he usually finishes work at five, then you should try to carry on until five-thirty, or later. If he normally takes an hour for lunch, you should take three-quarters of an hour when you are with him. If he doesn't like opening new accounts, spend the day opening new accounts. If he has difficult customers, you deal with them. If there is any call which seems impossible—YOU MAKE THAT CALL.

FOR SPECIALITY FIELD MANAGERS

Never ask a salesman if he has any prospects. Go out and cold canvass for new business. Only when you have obtained some orders, or made some good prospects for him yourself, need you attend to any of his prospects—and then only if he insists on your doing so.

YOUR CAR

If you have a car and your salesman has not a car, get to his territory, then park your car, and work on foot.

ORDERS—ORDERS—ORDERS

If you get a good order while working with a salesman, and you want to telephone head office about it, let your salesman do the telephoning. Let him receive all the praise. However little he has done towards helping to sell, do encourage him, by picking out one or two points which might have helped, and express the opinion that the few ideas he brought forward did materially help the sale along.

Never try to create the impression that the salesman could not have got the order without you. Always mention that he could have obtained it himself. That will give him confidence.

Build up your salesmen, and you will eventually build up a good team.

CAREFUL NOW

When working with a salesman you cannot be too careful over your selling. Never make any statement which could have a double meaning.

Never convey to a customer that you are granting a special concession. Whatever you do, the salesman will copy.

One sales manager told me that his field managers had the right to reverse the charge when telephoning head office about any important point. This they did on many occasions. Before long the sales manager noticed that all the salesmen on the firm—and there were over 100 of them—were reversing the charges from all over the country on any pretext whatsoever. They were copying their managers.

That's just a small point, but it will show you what I mean.

DO YOU WANT TO BE A SALES MANAGER?

If you want to be a sales manager then you have to do everything right as a field manager, and that means good liaison with your head office.

See that your reports are sent in to time. A salesman may moan about sending in reports, but a field manager must never do this.

See that your head office know where they can contact you at any time.

Make sure that you read carefully all the copy letters sent to you, and that you get salesmen to deal with any problem which you know head office have raised with them.

The more you help head office, the more likely it is that one day you will be at head office yourself.

YOUR TEAM

You have to sacrifice a lot to reach the top. To keep your team successful, you must understand your men. You must sympathise with them in their troubles, help them, and always be unselfish towards them.

If there is ever a question of your increasing your income, but by doing so a salesman might lose a little money, then think first of your salesman.

The success of your team depends purely upon what you are willing to do for them.

WIN THEIR ADMIRATION FOR THE WAY YOU WORK.

WIN THEIR RESPECT BY YOUR OWN INTEGRITY.

WIN THEIR LOYALTY BY YOUR UNSELFISHNESS.

CHAPTER XIV

One Hundred and Thirty Ways of Checking and Improving Your Sales Ability

It has been said that when a man passes middle age he should check up on himself, and then live in such a way as to enable him to get the best out of life. No salesman should wait until middle age before he has a personal check-up. In fact, to succeed, good salesmen should have some form of check-up every day.

The following check-up charts will help you to see yourselves as others see you. They will also help you to find your faults, and then to eradicate them.

SELF-ANALYSIS

One of the first sales lectures I ever attended took place at the height of the Freudian era. Everyone was talking about psycho-analysis, and its benefits to mankind. The lecturer on this occasion explained the advantages of psychology and analysis when used by salesmen.

Looking back now I see that he rather muddled the whole thing because, while he meant to imply that all good salesmen should analyse their sales effort, he inferred that anyone who tried to analyse himself could solve problems arising from his repressions.

I tried it on myself after the lecture. As I thought of all my faults and problems I became more and more depressed.

Self-analysis can be overdone. On the other hand, it is a good thing if carried out in the proper manner. Write down on a piece of paper all your faults—the mistakes you make in selling

—and then write down on another piece of paper all your assets. You will find that your assets far exceed your faults, and this will give you a great deal of confidence. If you don't do this you are apt to be too self-critical.

After you have made a sale, write down the mistakes you made; but also write down the good sales points you drove home. That will hearten you and increase your confidence, because you will realise that your mistakes were not so bad and that you put up a good display. It will make you feel all the better for your next sales effort.

Self-analysis is only good if you are fair to yourself and write down your assets as well as your liabilities.

ELEVEN CHECKS ON YOUR WORK

By working properly you can substantially increase your income, because it is a fact that few salesmen work to more than sixty per cent capacity.

You should make a daily check on these questions:

1. Do you make your first call as early as possible each day, and in any event not later than nine o'clock?
2. Do you work systematically?
3. Are you always trying to open new accounts?
4. Do you check up regularly in the local trade directories, at the local chamber of commerce, etc., to see if there are any newcomers to the district whom you have not contacted?
5. Do you try to get recommendations from your customers?
6. Do you cut down wasted travelling time as much as you possibly can?
7. If you have to deal with an enquiry, do you make plans to enable you to make your calls in that district, rather than make a long journey for just one call?
8. When you feel it is time to finish work, do you make that extra last call which so often results in business?

9. Do you always carry your samples with you?
10. Do you work every Saturday morning?
11. Do you try to do your correspondence over the week-end, so that no time is taken up during the working day with writing letters?

CHECK UP ON THESE POINTS EVERY DAY, AND YOU WILL IN-CREASE YOUR INCOME.

TEN REASONS WHY AN ORDER WAS NOT TAKEN

The salesman should check up after he has made a successful sale to see which points hit home, and to remind himself that these points must be emphasised at the next call. And he should also check up, when he loses a sale, to try to find out why the order was not obtained.

A check made from reports from one hundred and thirty area and district managers, allied to the answers taken from a questionnaire sent out to retailers and buyers, brought out the following reasons why orders were not placed, although the goods could have been sold and, in fact, were sold, when a different salesman called subsequently.

1. The salesman's appearance was against him and confidence was lost.
2. The salesman was too glib and obviously lacked sincerity.
3. The salesman made some tactless remark early in the sale which irritated the buyer.
4. The salesman, by trying to stress his own importance, had belittled the buyer.
5. The salesman did not tell his full sales story.
6. The salesman was obviously more interested in his sales story than in the prospect's business.
7. The salesman was not willing to listen to the prospect.
8. The samples or literature shown were in bad condition.
9. The salesman had been too familiar.
10. The salesman did not ask for the order.

THE FOUR WHATS

I read this in a humorous magazine: A boxer who had taken a bad beating for several rounds is in his corner waiting for the next round to begin. Before the bell goes his chief second says to him, "Right, I've got it! Now this is your plan . . ."

The boxer answers, wearily, "This is no time to make plans."

That remark could also apply to selling. You can't make plans when you are in the shop, office or factory, battling away for an order. They have to be made in advance. And when making your plans in advance it is a good idea to remember the four whats.

Answer them correctly and there won't be much wrong with your plan of campaign.

1. What is the reason for your making the call?
2. What would the prospect gain by giving you an interview?
3. What can you do to help him?
4. What would be the reason for his buying your product?

Check up regularly on the FOUR WHATS.

FIVE POINTS WHICH SCARE A SALESMAN

When the following points are raised don't be scared. They are only raised by the prospect because you have not convinced him and he wants to get rid of you. When you sell strongly you will hear these sentences less and less:

1. Put your proposition in writing.
2. Come and see me later.
3. I'll buy when trade improves.
4. I must ask my wife.
5. Leave me a leaflet.

Read these points carefully. Whenever you hear them you have not made a good job of your selling. Treat them as a warning that your selling must improve.

SIX HINTS TO THE HUMOROUS MAN

If you are good at telling a humorous story (and we all think we are) remember these six hints:

1. Never ridicule anyone.
2. You can always tell a story against yourself.
3. Don't try to be funny if the atmosphere is all wrong for funny stories.
4. In mixed company, don't tell stories which make fun of religion or of people's nationality.
5. Although you can tell a funny story, whatever you do, don't be a punster. A fellow who is continually making puns is nearly always disliked.
6. Don't keep a notebook full of funny anecdotes. If you can't remember a humorous yarn to tell at any given moment, then just keep quiet.

THIRTEEN MANNERISMS WHICH YOU SHOULD AVOID

1. Don't sniff.
2. Don't hold a handkerchief in your hand. When you have finished blowing your nose put your handkerchief away.
3. Don't let your lips droop at the side.
4. Don't stand too close to people when you talk to them. There is nothing nice about smelling another person's breath.
5. Don't hold the coat or jacket lapel of anyone to whom you are speaking.
6. Make certain that you don't suffer from bad breath. This is a MUST. Find somebody to check up on this for you and, if they tell you that you do suffer in this way, then purchase one of the many preparations which are now on the market to combat this condition.
7. Don't keep playing with your tie.

8. Don't play about with the prospect's ashtray, or anything on his desk.
9. Don't drum on the desk or table with a pencil or with your finger-tips.
10. Don't lean. When you talk to somebody, stand up straight.
11. Don't stand with your hands in your pockets.
12. Don't scratch a spot on your face.
13. Don't slap people on the back.

EIGHTEEN WAYS TO IMPROVE YOUR APPEARANCE

The salesman with a good appearance is always ahead of the man with a poor appearance. The salesman's appearance is his shop window. Here is the way to check up on yourself:

1. Wear a hat.
2. See that your hair is cut at least once a fortnight.
3. See that you shave every day (twice a day if your beard grows quickly).
4. Never wear a loud or gaudy tie.
5. See that your linen is clean.
6. Don't wear a handkerchief in your cuff, with the end protruding—unless it is the sort of handkerchief which is only used for show. There is nothing fascinating about a grubby piece of handkerchief half-covering a hand.
7. Don't put bulky articles in your side pockets.
8. See that there are no buttons missing from your jacket.
9. Have a crease in your trousers.
10. Don't carry a newspaper in your outside pocket.
11. See that your shoelaces are always done up tightly.
12. Wear your Sunday suit for your work. Most of your time is spent at work, so don't try to sell wearing a sports jacket and flannel trousers.
13. If you show a shirt cuff, see that it is not frayed.

14. Don't wear a loud tiepin, or any jewellery which could attract attention.
15. Do keep your shoes clean.
16. If you wear a pullover, tuck your tie inside the pullover, don't have it flapping outside.
17. Clean your finger-nails every day.
18. Always make certain that your hands are clean all the time.

Now don't say "What me?" because I *do* mean you. It doesn't matter how good an education you have had or how much interest you take in yourself—check up on these points regularly.

FIVE REPUTATIONS TO AVOID

It would do every salesman the world of good to spend a week or so at his head office. He would have to be there incognito or disguised, so that nobody would know who he really was. That would be the only way he would learn the true facts about himself.

Why is it that members of an office staff will go to endless trouble to help some salesmen, but won't lift a finger to do anything for others? It is because some salesmen build for themselves the wrong type of reputation.

Here are some of the reputations you *don't* want to win for yourself:

1. The reputation of being always ready to complain.
2. The reputation of never being on time with reports or replies to letters.
3. The reputation of always giving the maximum amount of trouble to those at the office. For example, arriving at the office just as it is closing down and insisting upon an urgent letter being sent that evening when, in point of fact, it wouldn't matter if the letter were not sent until the next morning. Or asking for shoals of literature to be sent to various customers, when the customers don't really want the literature and it is merely being sent to

bolster up your own morale. Making unnecessary telephone calls, etc., etc.

4. The reputation of being the type of person who never agrees with anything which is new.

5. The reputation of thinking that business is not a fifty-fifty proposition, but one in which the firm must always be prepared to give a little bit more than the salesman.

THE REPUTATION YOU WANT TO WIN FOR YOURSELF IS THAT OF BEING SOMEONE WHO DOES EVERYTHING RIGHT.

Fred Boyes, Northern manager, is now over sixty-five but everything he does is one hundred per cent correct, first time. He still fills in his reports with youthful energy. They are clearly written and just as clearly understood. He never leaves the firm in any doubt as to what action they should take—he advises them. He looks after his customers—he doesn't expect the office to do that for him. In all the years he's been with the company he's never been known to worry head office about anything whatsoever. He shoulders the whole responsibility of the job and, in consequence, has won a wonderful reputation for himself. So much so that over and over again I have heard other men say (managers as well as salesmen) : "If only I could be like Fred Boyes. . . ."

Well, they could! If they did everything that Fred Boyes does they would be just like him. Some men have tried, but after a week or two they slip back into their bad habits. The wonderful thing about Boyes is that he's been doing the same thing month after month, year after year. The fact that he's a top money-earner doesn't worry him very much. As he has so often said, "It isn't the money which matters, it's the job that counts. And if you do your job right, why the money must follow."

A GOOD REPUTATION MUST BE WON, AND RETAINED.

A TEN-POINT JOB CHECK

If you feel that you are not getting ahead fast enough with your present firm, check up on these points:

1. Is your job giving you a measure of happiness?
2. Have you confidence in your product?
3. When you began the job did you think that your advance would be more rapid than the success you have achieved?
4. Are you more interested in your hobby than in the work that you are doing?
5. Do you get along well with your sales manager?
6. Are you satisfied with your territory?
7. Do you feel the firm is giving you the backing you deserve?
8. Does your firm give good service to your customers?
9. Do you get on well with your customers?
10. Are you working as hard now as when you first started?

Check up on these points. If, after you have made a check, you discover that you are not doing as well in the job and you are not as happy in your work as you should be, then—no, wait a minute, don't start looking for another job. Just cast your mind back and check up on your previous job, and the job you had before that. Answer the same questions regarding each one of them.

Maybe you'll find that all along you have been blaming the wrong people for your lack of success. Perhaps it's you who are wrong.

THE FOUR-IN-ONE SALESMAN

Most members of an office staff do one job, and one job only. For example, the accountant looks after the accounts, the manager looks after the general running of the office, the cashier deals with the cash. A salesman, however, if he wants to succeed, must not look upon himself as being just a salesman. That is not sufficient to take a man to the top of the tree. A good salesman must be (1) a manager; (2) a secretary; (3) a cashier, and (4) of course, A SALESMAN.

He must be a good manager because he has to manage himself, and he has to manage his territory. He must be an efficient secretary because he must know the times of his appointments and he must be able to keep those appointments right on the dot. He often has to write his own letters—letters to customers thanking them for orders, letters to prospects advising them of a call. . . . So he has to know how to write a letter. He must be his own cashier, because he has to watch his expenses. He must plan his routes so that he does not waste money. And, at the end of every week, he must ask himself these questions:

Have I managed myself well?

Have I carried out my correspondence correctly?

Have I made the week pay for itself?

FIVE QUESTIONS

Here is a series of questions which every salesman should ask himself now and again, and he will continually be able to provide himself with the answers:

1. Do I know enough about the goods I am selling or the product I am handling to enable me to talk intelligently about it to any prospect?

2. Can I explain the points about my product so clearly that my prospect could resell that product if necessary?

3. As no product is perfect, what points about mine could a competitor criticise?

4. Do I know the trade terms relating to the product? Do I know the trade terms of the principal businesses I am calling on?

5. Do I know sufficient about my product so as not to be afraid of any questions that I may be asked about it?

This is a good list, and you will be well advised to check up on these points once every three months.

EIGHT IDEAS TO IMPROVE YOUR SELLING

The amateur salesman always overlooks the finer points of salesmanship, whereas the professional seeks to improve himself the whole time, and watches those small points which can make all the difference to a sale.

1. *Don't be a REPEATER*

Many salesmen adopt a stock phrase. Perhaps it may be, "You should do this, sir", and they 'You should' the prospect all over the shop during the whole sale

Check up on the next sale you make and, if you find you are using one sentence too often, then avoid it at subsequent calls.

2. *Be an ACTOR*

Every salesman, whether he knows it or not, is also an actor. If you see a first-class actor on the stage doing the simplest thing such as opening a window, or moving a chair, he appears to do it quite naturally although, in fact, he has rehearsed it over and over again.

The professional salesman has one or two gestures which add point to his sales talk. He also handles his sales aids in a professional manner.

If you fumble your sales aids, then spend an hour each night practising with them. A professional golfer at the top of his profession, if he should make a bad shot during a round, will spend at least an hour each evening practising that shot. Rehearse your part regularly.

3. *Check up on your POSTURE*

I don't expect any salesman to walk about the room with a book on his head so that he learns to walk properly. But too many salesmen stand incorrectly when facing a prospect. Either they lean too much, or they droop. Or, if asked to sit down, they slouch in the chair. The best posture to adopt is one of alertness.

4. *Don't be a BORE*

If you have a good sales point you must drive it home. You must often drive it home more than once—but don't keep on at it too long. Otherwise you will only bore the prospect.

5. Talk SLOWLY

Although the good salesman, once he gets excited, often talks quickly, most leading men are able to slow down their sales presentation. Most good public speakers do the same. Why? Because it gives them time to think.

Just talking will never get you an order. It is the sales talk which brings results. If you talk slowly, you can sense how each sentence is appealing to your prospect and you can work out in your mind—even while you are talking—what you should do next.

6. Don't be DEPRESSING

Every prospect has his own problems and worries, but he does not want to be reminded of them too often. Do try to be cheerful at every call. A prospect likes to buy from a man he feels is doing well, and cheerfulness is usually taken as one of the signs that a salesman is successful.

7. Alter your EXPRESSION

Too many salesmen never alter their expression when they are selling. They look the same when they finish the sales talk as when they started.

Don't be afraid to let your face light up when you want to smile. Don't be afraid to look clever by nodding sagely now and again. Don't be afraid to look really interested when the prospect is telling you something. Put over your sales talk to yourself in a mirror, and just see what you look like.

8. Use his NAME

Not one salesman in ten uses the prospect's name nearly enough. It cannot be stressed too often that this is the surest method of getting the prospect to like you quickly. The amateur salesman rarely uses the other man's name, but the professional uses it at the approach, and continues to use it throughout the sale.

Make it a rule right now never to go through a sales sequence unless you address the prospect by his name at least a dozen times during the sale.

IT'S ALL IN THE SELLING

A salesman wrote to me to tell me that cold canvass was not paying him dividends because it was not bringing results. I pointed out to him that cold canvass was only a means of confronting the greatest number of prospects in the shortest possible time.

When orders are scarce a salesman hasn't to look far to find the reason. He just is not selling well enough, that's all! There can be no other reason whatsoever. If we start from there we know where we are going.

In the *World's Press News* I read:

Selling needs hard, carefully thought-out strategy, rather than opportunist tactics.

That's very true, and yet only the top-grade salesmen understand what it means.

When a salesman isn't selling he asks himself, "What is wrong with me?" Then he supplies the answer—"Nothing is wrong with me. It's my goods, or my territory, which are wrong!"

Far better if he were to say, "Am I relying too much on opportunist tactics? Am I leaving things to see what happens when I confront the prospect?" If the answer to this is "Yes", then we can pinpoint the error right away.

To succeed, a salesman must leave nothing to chance. *He must make his plans carefully, and then adhere to those plans through thick and thin.*

Now I heard something else which appealed to me:

A first-class salesman is rarely a man able to produce a tremendous effort at a certain time during a sale, or able suddenly to overwhelm a prospect with some great selling idea which brings the sale to a close.

A truly great salesman is the man who is able to use a hundred or more very small average ideas—but to use them so effectively that the whole becomes an outstandingly good sale.

That, I think, is also excellent. If you break down a sale you find that there are hundreds of little things happening, odd phrases spoken, leaflets handled, which all go to make up a perfect story.

The average man overlooks these little things:

Careless handling of a leaflet can lose an order!
A sullen face can lose an order!
Grubby finger-nails can lose an order!
A hurried answer to an objection can lose an order!
Ignoring an assistant in a shop can lose an order!
Lack of a praise-giving sentence can lose an order!

And so it goes on. Firstly, are you an opportunist, or do you carefully plan your campaign before the call?

Secondly, do you watch over the hundreds of little things which take place during a sale to make certain that all those little points are so well put over that, in the end, you have produced the most perfect sale of all?

SIX SALES ANGLES TO AVOID

Every salesman must know everything about his product. In fact, until he knows more about it than the buyer he is never really confident. But when talking about his product here are some points which he must avoid:

1. Don't get involved in technicalities which the prospect doesn't understand. If you are selling technical equipment to a non-technical person, then you must simplify your explanations so that he can readily understand you.

2. If you are dealing with technical experts don't go over the same ground again and again. If he understands as much about it as you do he doesn't want to be bored by stuff he learned at technical college years before.

3. Don't show off. Don't try to prove to your prospect that you are a technical expert and that he should listen to the words of wisdom coming from your mouth. Rather make him feel that he is the expert.

4. Don't use your technical knowledge as a bludgeon to help you wipe out objections.

5. Never attempt to sell technically to anyone who hasn't the slightest interest in the technicalities of your product.

6. It is wrong to go into great technical detail with any prospect unless you point out continually how the technicalities of your product will be of benefit to him.

WHAT AM I NEGLECTING?

A good tip for salesmen is that they should ask themselves these questions at regular intervals:

Am I neglecting any special customer or type of customers?
Am I neglecting service after sales work?
Am I neglecting reports?

Find out what you are neglecting, and you'll find another way of increasing orders.

CHECK-UP CHART

1. What percentage of my customers won't see me?

Refer to your notebook or to your reports on your daily calls. Total the number of calls you have made in a definite period, then write down the number of calls where the receptionist or the commissionaire has barred your way. Now work out the percentage of wasted calls.

2. What percentage of buyers are not in the market for my kind of product?

Check up on your calls over a period to find out the number of prospects who told you that they weren't in the market for any product of the type you are selling. Calculate the percentage of this type of prospect.

3. *What percentage of customers prefer my competitors' products to mine?*

Check on a number of calls you have made to find out how many buyers would not buy from you because they preferred to buy from someone else in the same trade as yourself. Work out the percentage as against the total number of calls you have made.

Now, having calculated those three percentages, you can do something about increasing your sales quickly.

Question No. 1

If the percentage of wasted calls is high, then you must alter your approach technique to the commissionaire or the receptionist. And you have to do that quickly!

Question No. 2

If there are too many shopkeepers who are not in the market at all for products of the type you are selling, it means that you must find other outlets for your goods. A little research on your part should enable you to cut down calls on this type of prospect and find new stockists.

Question No. 3

If too high a percentage are buying your competitors' products and not yours, it means that there is a good market for the articles but you are not selling properly. You need not worry about finding out the advantages of your competitors' goods over yours. Obviously you haven't found out enough good selling points relating to your own products.

TO INCREASE SALES, CHECK UP ON THESE POINTS REGULARLY.

HAVE A DRINK

I don't believe you can judge a man by his face, but you can sometimes form an opinion of someone when watching him have a drink, or attempting to buy someone else one.

Here are some points worth watching in others—but most of all in yourself:

1. *The door-opener.* Here is a man who isn't normally very polite. He never opens a door for anyone, but when he enters a bar or public house he goes to great trouble to hold the door open while everyone else passes through first.

That is so that he can follow up in the rear and won't be the one to buy the round.

2. *The switcher.* If you're in a group and someone else stands the first round and you order a large Scotch whisky, that's all right —provided that when it's your turn to stand a round you stick to your Scotch. Don't when *you* have to buy the drinks, order a less expensive one for yourself.

3. *In a hurry.* If you are in a hurry to leave a party of four be sure that you buy the first round. Don't wait for three rounds to be bought and then suddenly decide you have an appointment.

4. *One of the boys.* Don't feel it incumbent upon you—especially if you are a new salesman—to get amongst the boys and have a few drinks. There are always salesmen who like to meet in the evenings and talk about their troubles over a drink. The trouble is that one drink becomes two, and two become three. Very few star salesmen want to be one of the boys. They only want to be men.

5. *Strong-minded.* If you are with a crowd and you don't want to drink, don't have one. It isn't weak to have a soft drink. If that's what you want, order it—and don't apologise for doing so.

6. *The teetotaller.* If you are buying a round of drinks and one of the men happens to be a teetotaller, order him a soft drink. Don't criticise him. Don't laugh at him. Don't make a joke about it. Don't ask him why he is teetotal. Just order the man a soft drink and leave it at that.

7. And, finally, here's a golden rule: NEVER, IN ANY CIRCUMSTANCES, DRINK DURING YOUR WORKING DAY.

It can never help you to get business, and it may even cause you to lose some.

No buyer likes to smell the breath of a man who has been drinking.

HOW TO INCREASE MY SALES

Some time ago I called in an industrial consultant to help me reorganise our business.

When we discussed the sales department I told him that I didn't think he could help a great deal here. His work, after all, was mainly confined to perfecting the office routine.

He asked me, "What makes you think that I couldn't help in your sales campaign?"

"I'm quite sure you could," I said. "But it would take a long time to study the whole problem, and then you should go out on the road to sell, to see the snags in practice."

"Let me read your sales manual," he said.

I gave him our sales manual to read.

A day or so later he came back and said to me, "Well, I've pinpointed three things that will enable any salesman to increase his turnover."

These are the points he put forward. He said that a salesman should ask himself these three questions every evening after returning home:

1. Could I sell to a higher percentage of prospects?
2. Could I sell more to each prospect or customer?
3. Could I sell a higher-priced article to each prospect?

After answering these questions, take the argument a step further.

1. Why can't I sell to a higher percentage of prospects?
2. Why can't I sell more to each prospect?
3. Why can't I sell higher-priced articles to each prospect?

When you have answered these questions, you will know how to increase your sales.

FINAL CHECK-UP

DO I PUT EVERYTHING INTO EVERY SALE EVERY DAY?

INDEX